QUICKBOOKS ABOUT ETSY AND PASSIVE INCOME:

The ultimate guide of Etsy business for beginners and Bookkeeping for Money-Making Machine

© **Copyright 2019 by Takeshi Kobayashi**

All rights reserved.

This document is geared towards providing exact and reliable information about the topic and issue covered. The publications is sold with the idea that the publisher is not required to render accounting, officially permitted, or otherwise, qualified services. If advice is necessary, legal or professional, a practiced individual in the profession should be ordered.

- From a Declaration of Principles, which was accepted, and approved equally by a Committee of the American Bar Association and a Committee of Publishers and Associations?

In no way is it legal to reproduce, duplicate, or transmit any part of this document in either electronic means or in printed format. Recording of this publication is strictly prohibited and any storage of this document is not allowed unless with written permission from the publisher. All rights reserved.

The information provided herein is stated to be truthful and consistent, in that any liability, in term of inattention or otherwise, by any usage or abuse of any policies, processes, or directions contained within is the solitary and utter responsibility of the recipient reader. Under no circumstances will any legal responsibility or blame be held against the publisher for any reparation, damages, or monetary loss due to the information herein, either directly or indirectly.

Respective authors own all copyrights not held by the publisher.

The information herein is offered for informational purposes solely, and is universal as so. The presentation of the information is without contract or any type of guarantee assurance.

The trademarks that are used are without any consent, and the publication of the trademark is without permission or backing by the trademark owner. All trademarks and brands within this book are for clarifying purposes only and are the owned by the owners themselves, not affiliated with this document.

TABLE OF CONTENTS

Introduction..1

Chapter 1: How To Price Products To Sell On Etsy.............10

Chapter 2: Is Selling On Etsy Worth It? 29

Chapter 3: Affiliate Marketing...39

Chapter 4: What To Sell On Etsy: 10 Questions To Help You Decide 51

Chapter 5: Best Selling Products And Categories.................58

Chapter 6: What To Do With Your Etsy Store When You Go On Vacation..70

Chapter 7: Why Your Etsy Business Needs A Website.........84

Chapter 8: Managing Your Etsy Account From Anywhere With Wimax 93

Chapter 9: How To Create Passive Income With Etsy 101

Chapter 10: 15 Reasons Why Your Etsy Shop Doesn't Get Much Sales..108

Chapter 11: 3 Reasons Selling Digital Downloads On Etsy Limits Your Growth...118

Chapter 12: Ordering Invitations On Etsy - Ensuring A Positive Outcome For A High Quality End Product 127

Chapter 13: How To Sell On Etsy Wholesale.....................134

Chapter 14: The Do's And Don'ts Of Selling Successfully On Etsy 143

Chapter 15: How To Sell Photos On Etsy...........................153

Chapter 16: International Selling On Etsy 168

Chapter 17: Running An Etsy Store In College..................176

INTRODUCTION

Etsy is one of the best ways to create an online craft business for a new seller. You can quickly and easily set up an online store without worrying about building your own website or setting up ecommerce on your own. In under an hour you can sell to a built in market of eager customers from all over the world! It just takes a little knowledge and practice to make Etsy work for you in building a successful online business selling your crafts. If you're just starting out on Etsy.

First some statistics: Etsy is the world's largest online marketplace for indie handmade goods and it is growing fast. $25.5 million worth of goods were sold on Etsy in August. That is a more than 7% increase over July, and a 75% increase over August of 2009! Etsy got 777 million page views in the month of August alone.

Here is how to build a shop on Etsy. First you have to visit Etsy and set up an account. It's free. You will choose one account name that will never change (so choose well!). But one account can have several shops so if you have more than one kind of craft business, you can divide up your wares into distinct stores with their own branding. Try to make a shop name that is unique and memorable!

Once you have your account and at least one shop, you need to set up your customer facing facade. You do this through "Your Etsy." Click on the interface for "Appearance" to start. First, you have to get a banner for the top of your shop. Etsy gives some banners however it's better to make your own. For good tutorials on making Etsy Banners and different parts of selling on Etsy, you can check the Etsy Blog, called "The Storque." They have "How-To" posts all the time that are really helpful. Also, there are great graphic configuration shops on Etsy who will custom design a standard for you for a small cost.

After your banner you will enter your one-line shop description, and also create a Shop Announcement, where you explain what you do and what makes your shop unique. You will also fill out sections on Shop Policies, which explains how you will handle shipping, and things like returns. Last, you will create a "Shipping Profile" that covers your domestic and international shipping rates. You can get an idea about how to do all these by checking other shops. It's not hard.

Once you get your shop set up, you can start listing items. Just click "list an item" to start. You give it a title (think about Google Search and put your keywords up front in the title--avoid whimsical or vague titles), and then describe it. Be specific. Include colors and measurements. Tell a little story about it what makes it unique. Then move on to materials, where you list what went into the item. Be careful to use commas between each material, and no periods or dashes. Then on the next page, you "tag" the item. You get 14 tags. Use them all! Tag with colors, especially trendy seasonal colors, seasonal themes like holidays, patterns (houndstooth, polka dot, etc.), shapes (square, chunky, etc.) and motifs (woodland animals is trendy right now, for example).

From that point forward, you ought to upload 5 photographs. Presently this is the important part- - your photographs have to be good! You can use your computerized point and shoot camera, however, make sure it's set on macro for closeup shooting (the large scale function is the little flower catch on most cameras). Get a decent simple background that has some intrigue to it. For example, photographs of your jewelry on pretty rocks or on a piece of wood. Take bunches of shots!

Then, and this is important, import your photos into photo editing software like Photoshop or even Picasa (easy and free), and tinker with them. Crop them to highlight and magnify your product. Sharpen them. Use highlights and fill light to brighten them, and use contrast to make your colors stand out. Remember that the tiny thumbnail photos that customers see when they're browsing are little squares so make sure your product is visible in a square version of your photo.

Finally, export your photos to a Pictures file in about a 1000 pixel size. Etsy won't take photos larger than 2 MB. You can upload your photos from there into Etsy.

After you finish uploading, you just click "finish" and agree to pay 20 cents per listing, and you're done.

Here are the fees: it costs 20 cents per listing, and then Etsy takes 3% of your sale. Paypal also takes 1%. So, price your items accordingly.

A note on pricing: don't price too low! The word on the street at Etsy is: if you want to sell more, raise your prices.

It is a good idea to have at least 20 items in your store, and more if you can. Someone did some research and found out that sellers who have twice as many items do more than twice as much business. In other words, having a well stocked shop makes customers buy more!

Now that you have your shop set up, it's time to promote it. Easy ways to promote are to use the Showcase Feature on Etsy (cost: $7), relist and add new items constantly (that way your stuff stays at the top of lists in your categories), and participate in the Forums that are on the "Community" section of the Etsy site. Join some Teams of other sellers that do similar work as you (find Teams in the Community section also). That gets your name out there.

Other ways to promote your Etsy shop are by posting your photos to free galleries like Craftgawker or ShowcaseEdge, setting up links to your site at resource sites like Unanimous Craft or Esellernow, and checking out membership sites like Handmadecraftshow and

Handmade Spark.

GETTING STARTED ON ETSY

Artisans young and old, regardless of their craft will find an audience and customers online at Etsy. What is Etsy, you ask? Etsy is an online marketplace for buying and selling all things handmade.

Etsy has been online since June, 2005 and now helps more than 100,000 seller's from around the world sell their handmade goods. If you sell handmade goods from candles to jewelry, pet products to food and even digital products then Etsy is a great way to expand your audience and boost profits.

Benefits of Selling on Etsy

·**Your own URL.** Etsy provides sellers with a customizable online shop which includes a URL based on your username, access to marketing tools and resources and the ability to participate in an online community of Etsy sellers who network and support each other.

·**Easy to use.** You don't need to know HTML to set up

shop on Etsy. Additionally, the majority of the transactions made through Etsy are conducted through PayPal making the payment and shipping process straightforward for both you and your customers.

·It's free to get started selling on Etsy.

Getting Started

To start selling on Etsy your first step is to register for a record. Getting registered requires including credit card information to your account, which they will then check. This card will be utilized to pay you're posting and exchange fees.

Much like eBay, Etsy charges listing expenses and a little exchange expense per deal. Posting fees are .20 cents to list an thing for four months and .20 cents for each additional thing. When your thing sells, you'll pay a 3.5% transaction expense.

Optimizing your Etsy Online Store

Because there are too many sellers on Etsy, it's important to make a name for yourself and stand out from the crowd.

- **Choose your username wisely**. Your username is what will become your store URL.

- **Make a positive impression**. Like eBay, sellers can build credibility through positive feedback ratings from customers.

- **Research your competition.** It's also critical to spend some time checking out the Etsy website, your competition, and other artisans. This will help you set prices, create your online store, and position your products competitively.

- **Take good pictures.** Because handmade items are unique items, it's important for your audience to be able to see your wares. This means taking great pictures. You are allowed five pictures per item - use the space and show off your handmade goods for all their worth.

- **Write detailed product descriptions.** It's also important to provide accurate and detailed, though not long winded, descriptions of your products. If your product has an interesting story behind it, share. Tell prospects what your products are made out of, their size and shipping options.

·Take advantage of tagging features and categories. Your customers and prospects search Etsy based on tags and keywords. As a seller, you're able to use 14 keywords/tags per listing.

•Cross promote. On the off chance that you have a business site, direct traffic to your Etsy site and vice versa. On your business website, collect visitor data and establish ordinary correspondence with prospects and customers to encourage rehashes deals and generate interest.

Etsy has turned into the premiere website for purchasing and selling all things homemade. Its growing rapidly and does not show signs of halting. On the off chance that you sell homemade goods, or are considering selling homemade merchandise, exploit of Etsy to reach an enormous and focused on audience and become your business.

CHAPTER 1
HOW TO PRICE PRODUCTS TO SELL ON ETSY

Pricing is often one of the hardest parts of starting an Etsy shop for a newbie seller. Crafters is frequently tend to underestimate their wares and underestimate the real cash and time that went into their creation. Or on the other hand, they feel that customers won't pay anything yet shake bottom prices for their work. In any case, learning to perceive the value and worth of the handmade things you make, and communicating that esteem through cost, is one of the most important steps a new vender can make to set their Etsy shop on a firm budgetary footing and construct a foundation for Etsy achievement.

This chapter will give a three point strategy for Etsy pricing. The first point will focus on how to compute your real costs in materials and time. The second point will focus on understanding your specialty market price go. The third point will focus on special pricing.

First, how to figure your real costs in materials in time. Well, start by including the costs of all the components in your creation, do not forget small, almost intangible items like glue, thread, paint, varnish, sealer, and so forth. Include an hourly wage for yourself that you think is reasonable.

In this way, state for example that you are making a necklace that includes $5.00 in globules, $2.00 in chain, and $1.00 in findings. Included that comes to $8.00. Now suppose that necklace took you 20 minutes to make. At $20 an hour wage, that comes to $6.67. Now your total comes to $14.67. Double that, and it comes to approximately $29.00. This is a possible fair price. In any case, ask yourself, what level of technical difficulty and preparing went into the 20 minutes of work? Is it something highly original that no one else knows how to do? Then raises your hourly wage and goes from there. Or on the other hand, conversely, is it a very simple design that is much similar to others as of now available. You may not be able to charge a premium for the creation of that item and the cost should be dropped.

This is where point number two, your specialty market

cost range comes in.

Thoroughly research your competition. It can be demoralizing to see how much beautiful work is on Etsy and how many sellers already have thriving shops doing things similar to yours. But don't despair! If your work is good and priced right (and promoted well), it will find a market. Look honestly at your pieces compared to the others already on the market. Are they equivalent quality? Equally important, are they photographed and staged beautifully so that they look desirable and must-have? If you can answer yes to both those questions, then study the average prices for equivalent items in the other shops, and aim for the high end of those.

Indeed, you read that right. Go for the top of the line. One of the privileged insights to selling on Etsy is, if you want to sell more, raise your prices. While the rest of the country may be in a retreat, handmade jewelry is still a boutique, luxury item, and deal prices don't work. In the event that clients wanted deal adornments, they could have gone to Target (which frankly, has absolutely cute gems for pennies). Your price shows your value and your quality. Resist the temptation to undersell. It won't support your business over the long haul.

Yet, be sure and provide incontrovertible esteem at that cost. Make your customer feel loved and appreciated by good communication throughout the transaction, a lovely packaging job, and instant customer fulfillment in the event there is any problem with your item or the sale. Clients pay a premium for the individual, handmade experience. That goes beyond the thing itself to the entire exchange.

SELL HANDMADE CRAFTS ON ETSY

Many people enjoy making a variety of types of crafts. The good news is that people can now make a substantial sum from their hobbies by selling their goods through Etsy, an online retailer. From handmade cards to origami, paintings, and even soap, there is a different type of craft for every person who wants to make some extra cash selling them online.

Etsy is an online company that allows people to sell their goods through their marketplace. You can create your own online store, upload photos of your crafts, and set your own prices. It is a very cost effective way to get your online retail business going.

You need to keep in mind that you can only sell handmade crafts on the site. The great news is that you can sell products in a variety of categories. Clothing, cards, ceramics, toys, jewelry, and more are all popular items that you can find when you peruse the site.

If you have a hobby and a passion for creating handmade crafts, you can sell online through Etsy.com and make money. With the right marketing strategies, as well as a good product of course, you can make a substantial income. I personally know two people who sell their handmade crafts on the site (a card maker and a soap maker) that make more than a thousand dollars a month on average.

Making good money with a hobby is something that most people dream about doing. Thanks to services like Etsy, it has become far easier to make that dream a reality.

CREATE AN ACCOUNT

Etsy.com reaches an estimated 11 million people monthly in the U.S. So what artisan wouldn't want to get in front of an audience like that? It's easy and inexpensive to get started. The hard part is making sales, but we'll get to that.

First, familiarize yourself with Etsy's sellers' requirements. (There are clear do's and don'ts on the Etsy site.) Then, look at other shops you admire to get presentation ideas and read through other sellers' stories to figure out what you want to say about your own profile and shop. There are also a lot of tips and valuable information right on the Etsy site.

Next, open an Etsy account. This will enable you to buy and sell. As far as sellers go, there are two categories: handcrafter's and collectors. Once you know which category you fit into, gather your products together. These are the items you are going to show in your shop. You can always add or delete products at any time.

Photograph, price, and write a description for each product and come up with a name for your shop. Again, research other Etsy stores, blogs, and to see what you like and what would be appropriate for your wares.

Now you're ready to "build" and "stock" your store. Create an eye-catching banner and avatar (symbol) for your shop. There are specific pixel and resolution requirements, which Etsy makes clear in their information section.

Once your product pictures, prices, and descriptions are uploaded onto the site, all that is left to do is put in keywords so viewers can search for and find your items. Then, you just sit back and wait for the money to pour in, right? Wrong!

You will need to check analytics to see how much interest your products generate and if your keywords are working. Be prepared to make adjustments, and be patient. It's a crowded marketplace and you have to find ways to make your products stand out. Good photography and accurate descriptions are crucial as are choosing keywords that people actually use.

Consider marketing your wares via the site's advertising venues, but also take advantage of free ways to promote your shop. Put a notation on your business card and a link on your email signature. Also, be sure to take advantage of social media sites such as Pinterest, Facebook, and Twitter to help promote your shop and specific products.

HOW TO SELL ON ETSY

Are you a crafter who has wondered how to sell on Etsy? Most people in the crafting world have heard of Etsy, but not everyone knows how to sell on an online marketplace like Etsy. Selling successfully on Etsy takes a little practice and know-how. A common mistake that almost every "newbie" makes is to think that just because you set up a shop on Etsy, the customers are going to come flocking! That is far from the case. Learning how to sell on Etsy takes some trial and error and a good understanding of how internet marketplaces for crafts and arts work.

It is very common for a newbie seller to set up their brand new shop, full of hope and enthusiasm, only to discover that weeks and months pass by without a single sale. The seller becomes discouraged, and lets the shop languish, and eventually quits. But this does not have to happen! It is possible to succeed on Etsy. But like all things it takes hard work and a willingness to learn.

There are five secrets to selling on Etsy that every new seller who wants to be successful must master: photographs, tagging, pricing, descriptions, and promotion. Learn these five secrets and put them into practice, and you will see a significant increase in traffic to your Etsy shop, and in time, more sales as well.

First and foremost, are your photographs good enough? In most cases, the answer is no. Even when you have worked hard on your photographs, chances are they're not good enough. Look at the front page of Etsy. Look at the crisp, clear, vibrant eye-catching, and professional looking photos in those front page featured shots. Those photos were taken by average sellers with little digital point and shoot cameras. The difference is, successful sellers know how to use the Macro setting (the little flower button) on their digital cameras to take ultra close up shots of their wares. They know how to stage their pieces in clean, uncluttered, sophisticated settings such as against rocks, or on a piece of wood, or most commonly, in a simple light box. (you can purchase a simple light box set that includes the box, colored backgrounds, two photography lights, and a small tripod, for not much money on Ebay, and it will be the best investment you ever make in your business.)

Successful sellers also know how to tinker with their photographs to make them effective marketing tools. Every seller, to be successful has to learn to use some kind of photo editing software. Photoshop is the most common but Picasa is free and simple to learn. Cropping is the most important step. Pull your product right up to fill the entire screen. Get rid of blank space around it. Then sharpen the image and play with the fill light and highlights and saturation and contrast until your photo pops. Export it in the correct file size for Etsy (up to 2 mb) and you are ready. Photos should be cropped square since that's what appears on the Etsy listings. Good photos get you into treasuries, which are collections of 12 items chosen by other sellers. Treasuries get seen by lots of sellers and buyers, so taking Treasury-worthy photos is key to your Etsy success.

Second comes tagging. Tagging means choosing keywords that are the terms that customers will type in for their searches in Etsy. You get 14 tags in Etsy, and successful seller's use them all. Tagging is a bit of an art form and takes practice. Be sure to refer to the "From the Merch Desk" monthly blog post on Etsy, which informs sellers of the coming seasons color and style trends and suggests tagging terms.

Third, pricing. Pricing is tricky. Price too high and customers will flee. Price too low and customers won't take you seriously. Look at your competitors---the sellers selling items very similar to yours. Aim for the general average of those prices....and then go higher. Here is the secret of pricing on Etsy: if you want more sales raise your prices. It's the psychology of the handmade marketplace. If you price your items a bit higher, they have an impression of value. Also, have a couple items with very high prices. Those make everything else look "reasonable," and buyer-friendly.

Fourth, descriptions have to be complete. Remember that customers can't pick up and handle your item. They can't ask you questions directly. So you description has to answer all of their questions. What is the size? The color? The shape? The feel? What are the exact dimensions, and can they be varied? What are its uses? If it's jewelry, is it good for daytime or evening, or both? What are the materials? Where did they come from? How were they handled? Is it a durable or delicate item?

Beyond all of these factual elements, though, it is good to tell a story. What inspired you to create the item? What feelings does it evoke? Where did it come from? How do you imagine it being used?

Last of all, promote. Even if you do the four things listed above to perfection, it is unlikely that your shop will grow without promotion. You have to get your shop name out to a wide audience. You need to create your "brand." There are paid and free ways to do this. The free ways include creating a Facebook Fan Page and actively seeking fans, and creating a Twitter account and regularly tweeting about your work and business. Starting a blog is an important way to build your brand and get exposure. Listing your business on free craft business directories like Unanimous Craft is helpful. Also, participating en-thusiastically on Etsy's own forums and teams brings you into contact with a wide range of other sellers, who are also buyers (and friends and families of potential buyers). If you sell jewelry, wear your jewelry everywhere you go and always carry your business cards.

One of the best ways to promote your business is to participate in large online forums and blogs related to your craft. By posting comments and contributions often, you build hundreds of links back to your business site, and make your shop visible to all the readers of those forums and blogs. Remember, those readers are already interested in your item, because they made the effort to come to that specialized site in the first place.

HOW TO PURCHASE PRODUCTS?

If you want to buy products on etsy, the following ways are the best ways;

1. Click the Add to Cart button found on the listing page for the item you want to buy. Etsy displays your shopping cart.

2. If you want to continue shopping, click the Keep Shopping button. (If you click Keep Shopping, you can

return to your cart at any time by clicking the Cart link along the top of every Etsy page.)

Got cold feet? No worries. You can remove the item from your cart by clicking the Remove link. You can also click the Contact Shop Owner link to launch a convo with the shop owner. This option is helpful if you have questions about the item.

3. Under How You'll Pay, indicate how you want to pay for the item.

Note that the options available here may differ by shop. Options include gift card or credit card (what Etsy refers to as "Direct Checkout"), PayPal, check, and money order.

Some Etsy seller's issue coupon codes for their shops. When a seller issues a coupon code, a special Shop Coupon Code field appears. If you have a coupon code for the shop you're buying from, you enter it in the Shop Coupon Code field and click the Apply button. Etsy updates your Order Total information.

4. If you want, type a note to the seller in the Notes section.

Adding a note is important if you want to make a special request or you have a unique specification. In addition, in their item descriptions, some sellers request that you leave specifics about your order.

5. Click the Proceed to Checkout button.

Note that the exact verbiage on this button differs depending on which payment method you choose in Step 3.

FIVE BENEFITS OF SELLING ON ETSY

Have been toying with the idea of opening up an Etsy shop to sell your wares? Etsy is an online marketplace where crafters and artists can set up a shop to sell their unique goods. It's also where shoppers go when they want to find handmade or creative pieces. The very spirit of Etsy is that it's an online community where crafters, artisans, and small businesses can sell without competing with the mass manufacturers in the consumer marketplace. Previously, the crafter's only options were to lease out a corner of boutique or set up a booth at an art fair to try to make sales. While these are both fine avenues, Etsy has opened the floodgate by exposing sellers to a wide shopping audience, boasting a whopping 24 million active buyers. The site also fosters a closer buyer-seller relationship by encouraging open communication rather than purchasing from a large, faceless website.

1. To sell your goods!

Whether you enjoy drawing, screen printing, crocheting, turning books into things, making socks for dogs, making lamps out of non-lamp objects, or an endless variety of other crafts, now you can make items and actually sell them.To people! For money! Spin your enjoyable hobby into a profitable business by setting up on online store. Instead of trying to spread word through your friends, family and coworkers that you're selling handmade scarves with cat ears, you can tell an entire audience of online shoppers. Which brings us to our next point.

2. Exposure

Instead of trying to forge a name for yourself on your

own, you'll be marching under the well-known banner of the Etsy name. Most people already know about Etsy, so it's easy to direct them to your shop. Plus, Etsy utilizes Google ranking so you'll have better search engine optimization (SEO). Meaning, if you open on online store, and someone tries to find it on the internet, it's far more likely to pop up in a search as an Etsy store than if you have an independent website. Etsy also offers promotion opportunities for a small fee if you want to boost business and exposure.

3. Earn extra income

An Etsy store is a great way to make some side cash. Statistics show that the majority of the site's shop owner's have other sources of main income and an online shop on the side as a way to bring in some extra money. Chances are whatever you're selling you enjoy making anyway, so you might as well earn some money crafting. The amount of time you devote to running your store will really affect the success of your shop, sort of what you put in determines what you get out scenario. You can totally throw a few items online and wait for orders to trickle in. But one the of the benefits of Etsy is that here's a huge network of users who offer endless tips, tricks and tutorials on how to grow your shop.

4. It's easy to use

Etsy has made it unbelievably easy to set up an online store and get your business going, and they're constantly making improvements that streamline the process. Beginning with setting up your shop and posting pictures of your items, to making a sale and shipping orders, there are tools every step of the way that make it a smooth experience. Customers can make payments right on the site without having to go through an external channel like Paypal. You can buy and print shipping labels right from the site that estimate shipping costs so you can avoid the line at the post office. Plus, it's far easier than setting up your own website with a shop page, and it's free to create. Etsy does take a small fee from each sale and transaction through their site, but it's a pretty fair trade for the ease of use and exposure.

5. Better for sales

You'll get perks with Etsy that you may not have on your own. First of all, your shop comes with built-in statistics that you can use to track your customer's experience. They'll show you how many sales you've made and which items are most popular. Additionally, your stats will show you how many visitors you've had to your shop broken down by days and peak viewing times. You'll also see how they found you and keywords they searched that led them to your shop. This information can be used to tailor which items you post and how you post them to steer sales. Etsy also allows you to offer discounts and coupons on your items to encourage repeat sales. These are just a few of the benefits of selling on Etsy. There are tons of tips and tutorials out there that will show you ways to make your shop the best it can be. Best case, you get to sell your expertly handmade goods for some cold hard cash! Let the sales begin!

CHAPTER 2
IS SELLING ON ETSY WORTH IT?

As Etsy continues to change their algorithm, update their rules, and grow, more and more makers are questioning if Etsy is worth it in 2019. Should people with Etsy shops continue to put the effort in them and for those who don't have one, should they start one?

Answer the following 10 questions for your business:

1. How do you prefer to sell?

First and foremost, think about if you're excited to sell on Etsy. Do you enjoy putting time into your shop or does the idea of starting an Etsy shop excite you?

First and foremost, think about if you're excited to sell on Etsy. Do you enjoy putting time into your shop or does the idea of starting an Etsy shop excite you? If the thought of Etsy fills you with dread, you're not going to want to put time into it and you won't be putting your best foot forward when you do spend time on it. That will be reflected in your results.

If you've been thinking about setting up an Etsy shop for a while but just can't get motivated to take the first step, maybe that's an indication that it's not the right platform for you, regardless of how much success others have had on it.

One important lesson I've learned from over a decade of running my own businesses is: there's no one size fits all.

It can be frustrating when you're following the steps that worked for another business and it's just not working for you.

But on the other hand, it's exciting. You can pave your own path.

You can make your own goals and you can achieve them in a way that makes you happy. Passion must be behind everything you do and only you know what sparks that passion.

2. What are your profit margins?

For any business to survive, it must have profits. And you must know how much you profit from each sale before you can make solid decisions for your business, such as which sales platforms to use.

Based on your profits, Etsy may be a better fit for your business than a sales channel such as craft shows.

For example, let's say last month you spent $100 on expenses (e.g. materials, Etsy listings, marketing, etc.) and your wages total $100. If you sell all the product you made for $200, you've earned your $200 back and can repeat what you did last month. There is no profit and no extra money to spend on more supplies, marketing efforts, sales channels, or wages.

If you earned $400 dollars from selling all the product you made, you'd have an extra $200 to play with next month. You could put more money towards products, marketing, and selling to earn more than you did last month. With that profit, you can also pay yourself more so you're not just an employee getting paid for the hours put in.

The expense of selling through Etsy is lower, and

lower risk, than selling at a craft show, so if you have lower profit margins, Etsy may be the better choice between the two.

Etsy is also a better choice when compared to selling wholesale, if you have low profit margins.

However, you may find that making sales through your own website is the best option and may not cut into your profits as much as Etsy does. You will be charged transaction fees either way if you're using a service such as PayPal or Stripe to collect payments online. However, Etsy charges a listing fee for every item, which you won't have with your own website. You will have domain and hosting fees when running your own website, but those may be lower than Etsy listing fees, depending on your business.

Know your profit margins and how much each sales channel eats into them to determine which is the best option for you.

3. How do your customers shop?

Think about the product you're selling, the market you're targeting, and how your target market typically shops for your product.

Are they likely to search online for your product or visit a store and buy it when shopping for other products?

Etsy won't be worth it for you if your typical customer doesn't shop on Etsy.

For example, let's say a vendor is selling high-end jewelry to be worn with evening and ball gowns. They're targeting women who are in their 40's to 50's attending galas, charity dinners, operas, etc. When shopping for a special occasion, most people go to boutiques or department stores so they can try on a gown and see it with all the accessories; the clutch, earrings, necklace, etc.

It's unlikely that a woman in her 50's is going to buy a ball gown and then go to Etsy to find high-end jewelry to go with it. She wants to see the jewelry in-person and try it with the dress before deciding on it. Selling that jewelry wholesale to high-end boutiques carrying special occasion wear would be a better option than selling it through Etsy.

4. What is your roi?

As mentioned in THE SUCCESS PLANNER, it's important to track how much time and money goes into each major task on your to-do list so you can determine if it's actually worth your time and money. That's a task's ROI; return on investment.

Once you're set up on Etsy, you need to track how many hours and dollars you put into keeping your shop updated, promoting your shop, communicating with buyers, shipping orders, etc. and how much money you get back from it.

If you spend $100 each month on listing fees, taking photos, creating listings, promoting those listings on social media, etc. but you only sell 2 items per month from Etsy and that results in $50 of revenue, you're NOT making a return on investment.

In addition, if you earn more than $100 in revenue from Etsy, you'd be making a return on investment. Then the question is; how much?

If you put $100 into Etsy in a month and earn $110 back from it, that's only $10 profit. Is all the time and money you put into Etsy worth $10 profit or would that

$100 be better spend somewhere else?

Know where your sales are coming from and how much you're profiting after the time and money spent on the sales channel is deducted.

You may find Etsy doesn't produce enough sales or profit to justify all the hours and expenses it requires.

If another sales channel brings you more sales and requires less time and money to make those sales, it deserves more of your time and money.

5. Do your products stand out?

Take a look at the category your products fall under and scope out your competition.

In most cases, your products will be competing with thousands of similar products.

If you don't have something that sets your products apart (aside from being "made by you" or being "your designs") you may have a hard time making sales on Etsy.

When there are several similar options to choose from, consumers will go for the cheapest, quickest, or most convenient option unless there's a valuable reason not to.

When you put all the work into getting people to your website, they're only seeing your products and aren't distracted by millions of other listings.

At craft shows, there are usually only one or two other vendors selling similar items to you.

Consider how your products will do when placed next to thousands of listings on Etsy. Will they catch eyes and encourage people to click or get lost in a sea of photos?

6. What are your computer skills?

Etsy makes it fairly easy to set up an online shop, especially when comparing it to setting up your own website.

If you want to have an online presence but you have minimal computer skills, Etsy is likely your best option.

There are several tutorials that will walk you through how to set up your shop and their interface is pretty user-friendly.

Like anything, it will take some time to understand the platform and become comfortable with it, but if you have limited time to do so, my suggestion is to go for Etsy over setting up your own website.

Once you become comfortable with using Etsy, you can ease into the idea of starting your own website.

7. How will you get traffic?

One thing is for sure; Etsy sellers can no longer rely on adding listings to their shop and watching views and sales pour in.

If you hate social media and other forms on online marketing, it's going to be hard to get traffic to your Etsy shop and may not be worth it for you to use the platform.

When selling online, it also requires you to invest time into SEO (search engine optimization). Etsy can help your listings show up in Google searches because Etsy has a good ranking on Google. However, within Etsy, they are constantly changing their algorithm and when and how a listing shows up on the platform. So although Etsy might initially help attract Google shoppers, it's easier to lose those shoppers to other sellers

It may take longer to get your own website to rank on the first page of Google but once someone lands on your website, your products aren't competing with millions of others just like them. You decide what appears at the top of the page and you can keep your shoppers focused on your products.

8. What are your goals?

Where do you see your business in the coming years?

Do you want a business that is 100% online? Etsy may be a good starting point and support for your online business.

Do you want to open your own store one day? Perhaps focusing on selling wholesale to retailers is a better path. It may also be more effective to start your own website so you can slowly start to build traffic to it and it's ready to go when you do open that store.

You will also have an easier time getting someone on your newsletter list when they're on your website vs. Etsy. Which is absolutely essential to your business.

CHAPTER 3
AFFILIATE MARKETING

You can make money from Etsy if you're not a seller, by becoming an Etsy affiliate. To be an affiliate, you'll usually need a website or blog and social media channels to enable you to promote Etsy.

If you don't have a blog but you DO have active social media channels with a good following, then I think it's worth approaching Etsy to see if you can become an affiliate without a blog. I'm not 100% sure what their stance is on this, but well worth a try.

How much can you earn as an Etsy affiliate?

As an Etsy affiliate, you'd be promoting Etsy products that you love and would recommend to others, through banner adverts and text links.

In terms of potential earnings from Etsy, you will earn a 5% commission for items purchased by existing buyers and for new buyers, the commission is 8%.

There is a 30 day cookie period which means that if a

visitor clicks through to Etsy from your affiliate link, you'll receive a commission on qualifying sales for up to 30 days.

Sounds good, right?

It gets even better at seasonal times of the year. November and December is a brilliant time to be an Etsy affiliate, because many people are looking for gifts for Thanksgiving and Christmas, so you can put together an Etsy gift guide that you think your blog readers will enjoy.

How to become an Etsy affiliate

To apply to become an Etsy affiliate, you'll first of all need to sign up to Affiliate Window, which is a great platform to sign up to anyway – it has a whole host of other affiliate programmes to apply to if you wish.

You'll need to enter some details about your website, blog and social media channels. You will have to make a minimal deposit when you sign up so Affiliate Window can identify you, but this gets added onto your balance straightaway and you'll get it back when you reach the minimum payment threshold. Once you're approved for Affiliate Window, you can then apply to become an Etsy affiliate.

You can apply to become an Etsy affiliate whether you're based in the UK or USA. Any products you promote are linked up globally as far as Etsy are concerned so it doesn't matter if your blog is UK based but your visitors are also US based.

Something to be aware of is at the moment, you can't be both an Etsy affiliate and an Etsy seller. So if you have an Etsy shop already, you won't be accepted.

What is Etsy Payments?

Etsy Payments is the easiest way to get paid through Etsy. With Etsy Payments, your buyers can choose their preferred way to pay, and you get all your payments in one place.

Can I use PayPal without Etsy Payments?

If you sell in a country that doesn't accept Etsy Payments, then you can sign up for PayPal using your own PayPal account. Funds from PayPal sales on Etsy will be deposited into your PayPal account.

7 EASY MARKETING TIPS FOR ETSY SELLERS

Do you sell your handmade crafts in an Etsy shop? Are you frustrated and overwhelmed trying to get more traffic? How can you get people to your little shop when there are thousands of others on Etsy vying for position? And, with the recent changes at Etsy, the floodgates of sellers' has opened, making it even harder to get noticed. Well, you're not alone.

Here are a few marketing techniques that I use regularly:

1. Social Media

DUH, right? Of course, we all know about social media marketing but are you doing it right? It's really a fine balance of providing your followers with useful information peppered with the occasional ad from you. Keep in mind, if all you tweet or post about are your sales, you will very quickly lose your followers. Instead, try a ratio of 5:1. Five great, informative or entertaining articles to One of your advertisements. Which sites are best? Good question. The big three are Facebook, Twitter and

LinkedIn but Pinterest is quickly coming to the forefront. Try marketing on three sites and see how it goes. You can always add more later.

2. Newsletter

Remember that email list of customers you've been carefully cultivating? You have been cultivating your email list, right??? Well, past - happy - customer's are your best friend! You've already 'sold' them so they're more likely to come back for more of your crafty widgets. Make your Etsy customer's feel special by offering them something exclusive like free shipping or a free gift with purchase. And if you don't have an email list yet, get on it! Lots of free or cheap services out there (i.e. Mailchimp).

3. Beef up Your Shop

Another DUH but seriously, it's amazing how many sellers don't bother to list their items correctly. That means: Keywords in your headline but make sure it doesn't sound fake. Awesome photos - it's the biggest selling tool you have. Thoughtful tags - how would you search for your items?

4. Get Involved

Etsy has a very active community. Join teams, engage in discussions, ask questions! Also Favorite other shops and do some Treasuries. All of these things bring attention to your shop.

5. Post Daily

It's better to list one thing every day than to list 7 things at once. Listing daily keeps your shop closer to the top in searches.

6. Market to Groups

Facebook and Yahoo both have special interest groups. Find some that allow occasional marketing of your Etsy items.

7. Craftori

Have you heard of it? Craftori.com is a site where you can post your items for sale. They have free and premium listings. The bonus is that Craftori will then tweet about your item. Double bang for your buck!

WAYS TO MAKE MONEY ON ETSY

From handmade to digital to vintage to supplies, you can find tons of craft-related and creative enterprises on Etsy. There are four very broad categories of things that sell on Etsy:

Handmade items, things like doll clothes, artwork, toys, quilts, jewelry, knitted shawls, soaps, and even edibles like candy

Digital products invitations, photo collages, custom posters, scrapbook layouts, and printable planners

Vintage items, clothing, shoes, toys, accessories, and small items like buttons and jewelry

Supplies yarn, fabric, wooden rings, rhinestones, sequins, candy molds, beads, twine, patterns and stencils, scrapbooking paper, etc.

Whether you do custom portraits, pet bedding, fancy iced cookies, garden stones, embroidery, or business card design, there's a way you can make money on Etsy.

Digital Products Are a Great Opportunity

Etsy has a reputation for handmade items and craft supplies, but one of their lesser-known markets is in digital goods. Custom signs and posters are one thing that people will flock to Etsy and find, but there are tons of other digital products available on the marketplace, too.

One of the benefits of Etsy for graphic design is that you can set your own prices. At the same time, one of the drawbacks is that your audience there might not be as big because not as many people think of Etsy as a place for business card designs or printable meal planners.

This could be a drawback if you don't want to focus much effort on marketing your Etsy shop, but it also means there's a lot of space for you to move in and get some great traction.

SHIPPING COST ISSUES OF MOST ETSY SELLERS

If you do have a background on something, journalism, photography, needlework, or woodwork among others, than you may already have an idea that you can actually market these types of products online. There are several platforms that you can use to sell your products to a larger market without having to put up a business place, since you can do it over the internet. You can do this by using Facebook, Twitter, Multiply, MySpace, and eBay, Amazon, or Etsy. However, for handicrafts, Etsy is the most popular platform as it's designed exactly for that purpose: to sell handicrafts and other unique art crafts.

However, you should know that some people on Etsy are having a hard time selling their products, and this is due to the fact that their shipping cost is too high. For example, if you are trying to sell cross-stitches, you might want to do a little research first. You may try adding an item to your card and choose the option "Everywhere Else" you will see the difference between the shipping cost to US and other places. You have to take note that international shipping can be very tricky and you have to be mindful of your buyer's money.

Take note that if you are selling from the US and your buyer is from an Asian country, it is only natural that the shipping cost would be higher due to the distance. However, it should not be the same for the buyers from the US. US buyers buying products from US sellers should get lower shipping cost, and you have to consider this when doing online sales. You have to be aware of the international shipping rate and of the local shipping rate as well. If you are from the US, then you should not charge US buyers with the same shipping rate as those from other countries.

If you are to check your shipping rates and the number of buyers you have made transactions with, can you imagine how much money your buyers have wasted for the shipping of your product when they could have gotten it in a lower shipping rate? And do you know how many US buyers you have lost because of the cost of your shipping? If you are to consider this, you would know that your business should have grown farther than where it is now, if you were careful enough to consider your shipping rates.

This is one thing that most sellers on Etsy should take into consideration. If your target market is the country where you are residing from, than they should be the first one that you have to consider when it comes to shipping rates. The rest of the buyers from other countries are your optional targets and your shipping cost should be based on the international shipping rates. If you can take this into consideration, than your business will become a hit now more than ever.

WHY DO SHIPPING COSTS MATTER TO ETSY BUYERS AND SELLERS?

If you are a seller whose costs are higher than average, then shoppers may abandon your product when they see the cost to ship it. Conversely, you may decide to stop selling something because it is prohibitively expensive to ship and reduces your profit margins!

As a buyer, you may only buy if free shipping is offered, but at the very least want to make sure you aren't getting ripped off by high shipping costs!

Shipping First Class With Stamps

One thing that you should avoid is mailing your items first class with stamps or through the post office. I totally understand that the cost of shipping through Etsy can seem prohibitive if you are just sending a paper label or some stickers that you could throw in an envelope for a few cents.

But this way does not give you any tracking or

protections because you can't prove you mailed anything. Should it get lost, or the buyer leave you a bad review that they never got it, you have no way to prove that it shipped.

Fixed Price Shipping

If you are selling like sized and weight items, it is possible to calculate a standard shipping price. This can reduce costs for your buyer or yourself, but comes with it's own problems.

If it weighs more than a pound, shipping costs will vary by the distance it has to travel. Additionally, each time the post office raises its prices you will have to go in and change every listing.

How to reduce shipping costs

If you are looking for a cheaper way to ship, you might want to consider educating yourself on Parcel Select, Media Mail, Priority Mail padded envelopes, Regional Rates and Flat Rate shipping!

CHAPTER 4
WHAT TO SELL ON ETSY: 10 QUESTIONS TO HELP YOU DECIDE

Choosing what to sell on Etsy can be a challenge.

Whether you're just starting your handmade business or you are simply adding new products to your existing Etsy store, its wise to think critically about the products you are considering selling.

So, with your product idea in mind, consider the following questions before deciding what to sell on Etsy:

Can you make it?

This seems like an obvious question, but I'm always surprised by people in Facebook groups who have started a handmade business with a product they haven't even made yet. If you haven't even opened your Cricut, you're probably not ready to start a vinyl decal business.

I'd suggest making your item many times before deciding it's what you will sell on Etsy. This will allow you to master and streamline your process and produce consistently-high quality items. You don't want to be working out the kinks when you are getting an order ready to ship!

Do you enjoy making it?

This is another seemingly obvious question. You wouldn't be thinking of building a handmade business around a product if you don't enjoy making it, right? Again though, some people want to sell an item because it looks easy to make or because it is in high-demand. Maybe a large profit margin is enticing you.

This is no way to build a handmade business. When those orders start rolling in, you're going to have to make them, and if you hate what you make, you're not going to want to continue with your business.

Can you find a sustainable and affordable supplier for your materials?

Sourcing materials is an important part of running a handmade business. You're going to want to see if you can get consistently low prices for your materials from a reliable supplier. It's one thing to use a 40% off coupon.

Can you expand?

Running a handmade business isn't always exciting, but there are ways to keep your products fresh and interesting. Does your product allow for different designs or variations? Think about the colors, sizes, shapes, uses, and designs that can be applied to your product.

While you probably don't want to use all of them at this very moment, chances are, you'll want to liven it up a little bit later. When that happens, it's good to know that you'll be able to do so.

Does it serve a purpose or fulfill a need?

Think about why people will purchase your item. Does it serve some kind of purpose? The more specific the purpose, the more likely it is that people are going to purchase it. Don't get me wrong- maybe your product brings beauty into the world, and that's it purpose. That's valid. But when you're starting out, you want to be clear- which people will find it beautiful?

In fact, if you're struggling to determine what purpose

or need your product fulfills, think of your ideal customer. Who exactly will purchase this, and why?

Are the market conditions favorable?

Do some market research before you decide to build a business around a particular product. Are people searching for or purchasing this item? Use EtsyRank, the Etsy search bar, Google Keyword Planner, or the Keywords Everywhere Chrome extension to get a gauge of how many people are searching for your item and what that competition looks like.

You're looking for something that is in demand but that not too many people are already selling. If you find that you're making something in a saturated market, think seriously about how you can differentiate yourself. How can you make something that is just a little bit different?

Can you legally sell it?

If your product uses licensed characters, sports teams, brands, etc. You cannot sell it. Even vaguely associated products are off-limits.

Also don't copy other people! It's just not creative.

It's equally important to consider the law for the specific thing you make. Are there any special rules for products in your category? Children's items, bath and body products, and food are some categories that may require additional labeling or special considerations.

How will you ship it? (Or haul it to a craft show)

How much does your item weigh? Go ahead and use a postal scale to weigh it right now.

Now, what is you plan for packing it up and shipping it across the country? What boxes and packing supplies will you use? What shipping service? How much will this all cost? Will your customers be willing to pay that cost?

If you make large, heavy, or oddly-shaped items, it's not impossible. You'll just have to get creative.

If you're considering selling this product at craft shows, you should also think about how you'll get it there. Do your items fit neatly in totes that you can lift yourself.

What is your price point?

To determine your price point, first do some calculations. Exactly how much does it cost to make this item?

And how much time will it take for you to make one of these items? Once you have these numbers, you can determine your retail price. There are so many formulas for pricing out there. Try out a few, and see what you come up with.

Now do some market research. What are people already paying for this type of item? The goal is not to undercut other Etsy sellers. This doesn't help anyone, and you won't be able to continue in this way for long. Do, however, see if your price fits within a range of prices that customers seem willing to pay.

If your item costs $40 to make, but everyone else seems to be able to sell it for $15, you're going to have to somehow justify your costs to potential buyers or take a hard look at the price of your supplies.

How will you market it?

What is your specific plan for selling this item? Will you use an email list? (Excellent.) Or are you going to try to rely on social media? (The conversion rates for social media are actually pretty low.)

Additionally, put some thought into how you will

design your listing. Who will you target in your listing description? And how will you photograph your item?

Deciding what to sell on Etsy can be a challenge, but putting some thought into it will ensure that you have started your business in a way that is sustainable, profitable, and enjoyable for you.

CHAPTER 5
BEST SELLING PRODUCTS AND CATEGORIES

What are the Etsy best sellers? Have you considered creating an Etsy store but you're not sure what to list? Etsy is a great opportunity for arts and crafts experts' to break into the eCommerce business. It is an online eCommerce portal site that accepts all types of sellers. The only criteria are that you have to create the item yourself or produce it in its sellable form yourself. If creativity is a big part of your life and you have always wondered what to sell on Etsy to make this creativity profitable, this article will try to give you a starting point.

What to Sell on Etsy

The hardest part of deciding on an eCommerce venture is to choose what to focus on. Etsy has thousands of items in several categories, and they allow you to sell in the following categories for their platform:

1) Home and Living

Some sellers on Etsy.com focus on things for your home. From handcrafted pots for plants to home decor of all kinds, many sellers have success in this category. If you have a knack for selling home decorative items or interior design products, this may be a great category for you to explore.

2) Jewelry

Jewelry is one of the hottest-selling categories on this eCommerce site. People all over the world sell various jewelry items in this category, and many of the pieces are handmade.

3) Clothing

Handmade clothing items are also a favorite selling category so if you have a knack for sewing or embroidery, Etsy may be a good platform for you.

Most of the clothing items feature personalized names or accents that allow you to customize the clothing for specific customers. Many of the T-shirts sold in this category are vanity statements or declarations about popular trending topics. Some sellers purchase white T-shirts, then decorate them in ways that people like to sell on Etsy. This category also features many accessories such as belts, bags, and other items, as well.

4) Toys and Games

The Toys and Games category features a variety of handcrafted toys and games for all ages. From baby items to electronics games, you can sell many different items in this category as long as it qualifies as a game or toy.

5) Craft Supplies and Tools

Instead of selling completed items, some people focus on selling craft supplies and tools to enable others to create things for Etsy. This is a lucrative category if you have a supplier that can keep you furnished with many supplies. From candle-making supplies to doll-making and many other hobbies, you can be the go-to person that people turn to in order to find supplies to create their craft items.

6) Kids and Baby

This category is popular because it offers a wide variety of products that are handmade or created for children and infants. These items make great gifts, and many mothers of infants or others come to Etsy to look for these types of products.

7) Vintage

The Vintage category is dedicated to featuring all sort's of older or antique items. If you have older items that you have restored or antique dishes, for example, you can sell them on Etsy in the Vintage category.

Top 8 Best Sellers On Etsy

Now that you have the 7 most important categories on Etsy, you may be interested in knowing what the most recent 10 best selling items were. Below is a list of the latest Etsy best sellers.

1) Stickers

Believe it or not, kids stickers are the number one selling category currently in Etsy. The only requirement is that they have to have been made by the seller in some way such as applying the design or creating the product in some way. Etsy's format is unique because of its original craftsmanship so just make sure that you have a hand in creating what you sell. Stickers sell well because teachers, parents, and non-profit organizations often look for handcrafted stickers to buy in bulk that can serve as rewards and incentives for kids.

2) Handmade kids' clothing

Kids' clothing that is personalized or adds a unique touch is a big seller on Etsy. The concern about getting cute and trendy cloth for the kids is quite new, about few decades, and the market is booming right now. Plus we all know that people are ready to spend more to have personal items, this is even more true concerning kids clothing category (How can you resist to so much cuteness?). Also personalized kid's clothing make great gifts, which brings even more customers than just parents to those stores. So remember to propose something that is unique for your customers and that will make the item very personal to them.

3) Homemade or Specialized Candies

Homemade Sweet, a jelly bean, and specialized candy store offers sweet treats that you cannot find in a regular candy store. They are wrapped in unique wrapping to give them a distinctive flair.

4) Party decorations

Party decorations go over big on Etsy. Why? Because people don't want to have to drive to a party store and they enjoy browsing through the hundreds of party items available on this powerhouse supplier's site. Plus, one more time, customers can ask for personalisation. People that are throwing parties are doing for a reason: they want them to be memorable! Personalization help them reaching that goal.

5) Vinyl & heat transfer supplies

Just like the personalized clothing items, plastic, and heat transfer supplies are also a big seller on Etsy. Just like for jewels pieces and beads, this come probably from the fact that Etsy craft seller's buy vinyl and heat transfer supplies in order to realize their own creation and sell them on their stores. The platform is aware of this fact and reacted by launching another marketplace called Etsy studio, made for craft items suppliers.

6) Unique items

Items that are hard to find in brick-and-mortar stores can become Etsy best sellers. That's because people who deal with arts, crafts and jewelry have come to realize that Etsy is now the go-to site to find these rare or hard-to-find treasure.

7) Vintage items

Vintage items have a great success on Etsy because they are not easy to find. Because of their scarcity, people are ready to pay the price. Authentics vintages items are usually sold in junk shop and collectors have to travel a lot in order to find them. Etsy vintage category makes the searching process much more easier for them.

8) Hard-to-Find items

Finally, offering anything unique that is hard-to-find can help you to create a steady income for your Etsy business. If you provide access to items that cannot be found elsewhere, you may be rolling in dough soon. It can either be some really hard to find antique items, but don't forget that Etsy is a marketplace for creative people before everything else. This means that you can create whatever rare items you desire since it will be your creation only. Think well about the niche market you could fit in and take the leap.

DROPSHIPPING ON ETSY

There's been some buzz about Etsy dropshipping lately. Dropshippers have been looking to promote trending products and find new products from different marketplaces, which makes dropshipping on Etsy – as well as sourcing products from Etsy – seem attractive. And with Etsy's 2.1 million sellers, the marketplace appears to be a goldmine for quality products. But could Etsy dropshipping be too good to be true?

What is Dropshipping?

Dropshipping is a business model where a merchant sells products without needing to manufacture goods, carry inventory, or ship products to customers.

The business model is popular among new and risk-averse entrepreneurs who want to start an ecommerce business.

Traditionally, entrepreneur's were required to buy products in bulk, at wholesale prices. If a product sold, great! If a product didn't, you're left with a box of unsold inventory.

Why? Well, for starters, you buy products from supplier's on an individual basis. So if a customer places an order on your store, you then order that product – and only that product – from the supplier, who will take care of the rest: manufacturing, picking, packaging, and shipping your product. So, not only do you save money – you also save a ton of time.

Etsy Dropshipping Cons

While Etsy dropshipping has some pretty cool benefits, their cons can make you reconsider the platform. Here are just a few of the Etsy dropshipping cons:

Retail price of products is high: The prices listed on Etsy are above retail value. For example, say you buy a bridal tiara on any traditional online store, you might pay around $91.97 for a really nice one (at least that's how much I paid for mine – you can even see the review I left on their page). However, the exact one I ended up buying cost $153.02 on Etsy. That's over $60 more than what I paid. Most online retailers buy products at wholesale prices. However, Etsy's pricing is often far above market value, making it unattractive to the average shopper. Especially a shopper who has the time to do some extra research.

Pay a listing fee: One of the biggest downsides of Etsy dropshipping is the listing you fee you have to pay to add a product to their marketplace. Listing fees are 20 cents per listing. But there's a catch – Etsy listings expire after four months. So you have to keep re-adding your listing to their marketplace, adding more manual work than it's worth. And you pay for the listing fee each time your product sells. If you use an ecommerce platform like Shopify, you can add products to your store without worrying about listing fees. Plus, your products stay hosted on your website for as long as you'd like.

Your dropshipping capabilities are limited: Etsy's seller policies don't specifically mention "dropshipping." Etsy does say, however, that reselling is allowed in some instances: "'Reselling' is selling an item that you, the seller, did not make or design." (This doubles as a more or less spot-on definition of dropshipping.) "Etsy's marketplace includes handmade items, vintage items, and craft supplies. Reselling is only allowed in the vintage and craft supplies categories." So you can resell/dropship, but you'll be handcuffed.

Etsy isn't sustainable: Maybe you're not looking to sell products on Etsy but from Etsy. That has some pretty serious disadvantages, too. If you want to dropship Etsy products, you'll find that the products that you can dropship don't sell well. And if you find that big, life-changing winning product, your Etsy supplier won't be able to sustain the business. A full-time, massive manufacturer can handle thousands and thousands of orders every day. But a handmade product by a part-time Etsy seller can't handle that same volume level. And so you'll never really score the jackpot you're looking for.

Wholesale option got shut down: Take a look at this update on the Etsy Wholesale program. In June 2018, Etsy made the decision to shut down their wholesale program, which allowed sellers to sell to retailers. Again, dropshipping on Etsy is still possible, but the platform has made moves that might make dropshippers nervous about future policy changes.

Etsy Dropshipping Rules

In it's "What Can Be Sold" section, Etsy explains, "Etsy is a unique marketplace. Buyers come here to purchase items that they might not find anywhere else. Everything listed for sale on Etsy must be handmade, vintage or a craft supply." They even clarify that the handmade goods must also be "made and/or designed by you, the seller."

When it comes to selling vintage products, they need to be at least 20 years old to be labelled as vintage. And when it comes to craft supplies, you can sell them from another supplier. However, you must disclose where you got the products from and their environmental attributes, such as if it's made from recycled material.

CHAPTER 6
WHAT TO DO WITH YOUR ETSY STORE WHEN YOU GO ON VACATION

Going on vacation, or doing an inventory audit is always a worry for the Etsy seller. Worry not, as here is some helpful advice to decide what to do with your store while you are away.

Etsy has a convenient "vacation mode" which allows Etsy sellers to put their store on hold with the click of a button. This is an "official hold", wherein no listings will show up either in the shop or in the category listings. It comes with a paragraph area where you may list a "vacation announcement" to explain to your customers the situation ie; on vacation, will reopen soon.

This option comes with an "auto-reply" to conversations where you can specify a special message, and even allows potential customers to sign up to receive an email for when your shop is reopened.

Etsy suggests doing this when "on vacation for an extended period of time." So what would be the harm in leaving your shop open during a vacation? What is an extended period of time? You must weigh the pros and cons and decide what best fits your shop.

If you are a seller that ships only once per week, and this is clearly listed in your announcement and decide you are going on vacation for only a few days, there is no sense putting your store into vacation mode. Ship the items when you get back, and update your announcement to reflect your next shipping date.

If you are that same once-per-week shipping Etsy seller going on vacation for two weeks, you may want to put the shop on hold the first week only, then reopen it for a week, so that when you get back the following day you can ship your items, essentially, still on schedule. A blurb in the shop announcement helps.

If you are the same once-per-week shipping Etsian, and going on a month long trip, it is recommended to put your store on vacation mode, at least the first three weeks, reopen on the last week with proper announcement information, essentially still on schedule.

If you decide to keep your store open for several weeks to a month long hiatus, you run the risk of alienating new buyers who are upset they have to wait so long to ship, so I would advise using the vacation mode in full, or half way during your vacation.

If you choose to not use that advice, and leave your store open during any vacation, it doesn't hurt to make a special "eye-catching banner" that informs customers your next shipping date. In addition change your "purchase confirmation" (thank you message) that goes to buyers upon purchase and include the next shipping date. Make sure to put this in the announcement clearly.

UNDERSTANDING HOW PAYPAL WORKS FOR ETSY SELLERS

PayPal plays two main roles in the Etsy storefront for Sellers. It is important to understand both options.

First, PayPal serves as an option wherein Sellers may pay their monthly Etsy bill (incurred for billing, transaction, and re listing fees) instead of using the credit card on file. By simply choosing this option when paying the bill, the money will be automatically deducted from the

PayPal account on file, using any backup methods on file with PayPal, should there not be enough funds available in the PayPal account.

Secondly and most important, Buyers may opt to pay Sellers with PayPal for their purchases. When setting up the Etsy shop, it is highly advisable to offer this option as many potential Buyers look for this option. Not to mention PayPal is a secure method of payment and has a Resolution center to resolve issues. Understand there is no fee from Etsy directly for using PayPal as a checkout option, however PayPal will charge appropriate fees on funds received.

An advanced feature for sellers with Merchant PayPal accounts it the ability to print and ship from the PayPal console. This easy to use shipping option includes discounted USPS or UPS account rates. UPS rates may take time for approval and discounts are based on packages sent per week. In addition to discounts, this option allows the Seller to print automated postage labels for most of your packages, and freebie benefits such as free delivery confirmation on some priority USPS mailings.

WHY FEEDBACK IS SO IMPORTANT ON ETSY

Are you wondering how to increase your sales at Etsy shop? Are you getting good traffic but not seeing the sales that you'd like? There are many aspects to increasing sales on Etsy, but you may be overlookinJHg the importance of feedback to converting traffic to sales on Etsy.

Feedback is when the buyers and sellers you interact with on Etsy rate your transaction. As a seller, you are hoping that your customers provide positive feedback. Your shop's feedback is featured prominently on your shop's main page, and it is often one of the first pieces of information that a potential custom looks at. Shop feedback has two parts: the number of feedbacks, and the percentage positive. In both cases, the higher the number, the better. Most successful sellers have 100% positive feedback.

The reason that positive feedback is important is that it gives customers confidence that you are an experienced and successful seller. Since buyers can't meet you personally, or walk into your shop, the feedback is their main evidence that you know how to treat your customers well.

There are six aspects to an Etsy purchase from start to finish that an Etsy seller should pay attention to if they want to get the most positive feedback possible from customers.

First off, you should have good products that are well presented and that customers want to buy.

Second, you should answer as many questions as possible in your shop policies about the nuts and bolts of your business, such as shipping schedules, returns, and refunds, so that customers feel they can buy with confidence.

Third, it is great to quickly and enthusiastically respond to any questions about your products from potential customers, which builds a relationship of trust.

Fourth, once you make a sale, acknowledge it with an email thanking the customer and giving a timeline for delivery.

Fifth, ship as quickly as you can, with attractive and

secure packaging. Customers in the internet age want instant gratification, so check your shop daily for orders.

And 6th, be committed to customer satisfaction. If something isn't perfect, make it right! Sometimes just acknowledging a mistake or flaw can do more to build trust (and future sales) than anything else.

Doing all of these things builds the kind of relationship of trust that encourages positive feedback. They are all good business practices and will form the foundation of a successful Etsy business in time.

But, many times even very satisfied customers don't take the time to do feedback. It takes a little extra time and effort, and sometimes customers don't remember. The average feedback rate is actually under 50% of all sales on Etsy.

So, a little extra incentive is key. Here is a secret tip that may increase your feedback rate well above the Etsy average. When you send your email acknowledging the sale (4 above), offer a discount code for a future purchase to your customer if they complete feedback after receiving their item. The discount can be whatever you like, but if you are a new shop with very few ratings, a nice big discount can work wonders. An offer of a good discount is a powerful incentive to your customers to remember to provide feedback for your transaction. The advantage of this practice is that it also provides an incentive for future sales, so that your shop gains more feedback and more sales as well.

ETSY'S NEW STAR RATING REVIEW SYSTEM

Etsy intended to promote honesty, fairness, and transparency across the marketplace, the new Review System allows buyer's to give a star rating to individual items they purchased. Now, instead of leaving Positive, Neutral, or Negative feedback, Etsy customers will leave a star rating for sellers ranging from giving a one star rating if the customer was disappointed with their purchase to a five star rating if the buyer loved their Etsy purchase. All old store feedback was automatically churned into star reviews by Etsy as follows:

- Positive feedback = 5 star rating

- Neutral feedback = 3 stars rating

- Negative feedback = 1 star rating

No more feedback for buyers

With the new shopper-friendly Review System, only star ratings from buyers show up on the store's reviews rating. On the flip side, all feedback that sellers used to get if they bought something from other Etsy stores are gone forever since sellers will no longer be able to leave feedback for buyers. This came as a shock to most sellers who can no longer leave feedback for buyers and who also saw their feedback score drop and only the number of reviews by buyers remained. However, this is a huge benefit to shoppers who now can exclusively see just the seller's feedback which will help shoppers evaluate a store before buying. But a review system that supports the buyer more than the sellers has Etsy store owners concerned.

No more buyer appreciation photos

Customers used to be able to share an appreciation photo along with their feedback to the seller, usually to show a product happy in its new home. However, this feature is gone with the new Review System so if you want to save your appreciation photos from your past customers, go to your Appreciation Photos and save them now so you can share the photos elsewhere like on your website or blog outside of Etsy. Your past Appreciation Photos from old buyer feedback will only be accessible until the end.

No more blank feedback

All reviews left by buyers must write at least five words in their review along with a star rating whereas before, buyers could leave a Positive, Neutral, or Negative feedback without writing any supporting reasons why they left that feedback. Now, new and future customers can read your juicy reviews and be even more inspired to shop with you.

Really old reviews don't matter

Ever get a Negative feedback a long time ago that has tarnished your feedback rating ever since? Good news! That Negative feedback will no longer haunt you! With the new rating system, your shop review score is an average of all your item ratings from the past 12 months and any reviews older than a year are not calculated in your current overall shop score. Etsy now displays your shop's star rating along with the total number of reviews your shop received since the beginning. On the left sidebar of your main shop page and on the Reviews tab under ever listing picture.

Reviews can be edited

Feedback left by Etsy members used to be permanent but now, reviews can be edited up to 60 days after the buyer received the item. The 60 day period starts after the buyer is scheduled to receive the item based on the estimated shipping and processing time. This ability for buyers to edit reviews is especially advantageous to the seller if you received a low rated review. This allows you to contact the buyer to resolve any outstanding issues so the buyer can give a higher star rating that reflects the resolution.

HOW TO GET THE MOST OUT OF YOUR ETSY SHOP

Etsy is one of the most popular places for crafters to start selling their handmade crafts online. It provides a market place for crafters and artists to sell their creations, vintage items and supplies.

But with over 300,000 different shops on Etsy how do you make your craft business stand out from the rest? How do you let your customers know your products are what they have always been looking for? How do you get found amongst all of the other stores? The following 10 tips will help you on your way to creating your best Etsy store.

1. Avatar and Banners - You only get one chance to make a first impression so they say, so make it count! Your shop banner is how your customer makes a judgement on your craft business and what you're selling so make it as good as it can be. Use your banner picture to show what you sell by including one of your products. Banners need to be exactly 760 pixels wide by 100 pixels tall or the image will be blurry. If you can't make one yourself on a programme like photoshop there are people on Etsy who'll make one for you.

2. Profile - Make sure you fill it in. No one likes talking about yourself but this is really an important step in the Etsy process. Let people know what is special about you and why you love what you make!

3. Photos - When you have decided what crafts to sell you'll need to get snapping! Make sure your photographs do your crafts justice. There are 5 spaces for your products on Etsy so use them ALL to show different angles and close ups of your items. Make sure your photos are well lit and in focus.

4. Create a Story- In your description, as well as giving the basic facts on size, measurements etc. Create a story around your craft to draw your customer in. Let your customer know how much love you put into your cool craft creations and your reader will feel more of a connection to your product. Write as if there is no picture.

5. Communication - Make sure you answer all enquiries promptly and courteously and have your contact details available for your customers.

6. Keywords - Give as much detail as possible in the titles of your listings. Think about what your customer is searching for. You need keywords in your title, description and tags.

7. Ship Overseas - You just have to do this if you want

to be successful on Etsy. We live in a global community and your customers are all across the world so you need to provide international shipping. Ask at your local post office for a list of shipping weights and costs to help make it easier to calculate.

8. Offer refunds - Nothing turns a customer off more than a 'no refund' policy. It makes you seem, well a little dodgy. You should fill your customer with a sense of confidence in your product, by offering a refund which can be easily sorted through pay-pal automatically.

9. Increase your inventory- You should aim to have around 100 items up for sale in order to be ranked well in search engines. The more choice you have the more opportunity you give your customers to find something that they like.

10. Packaging- Your marketing doesn't end once they've bought your product. Remember to be thoughtful in your packaging. Think of what you would like to receive yourself. Do you have a theme in your packaging? Use a cool craft paper to wrap your products up or add a small free gift. Include a business card and a thank you note. It's the little touches that will make you memorable.

CHAPTER 7
WHY YOUR ETSY BUSINESS NEEDS A WEBSITE

Since it launched 13 years ago, creative marketplace Etsy has helped turn countless creators into successful entrepreneurs. Its easy to see why. As of 2017, more than 1.93 million sellers used Etsy to sell their products, and nearly 33.4 million buyers had purchased goods through the marketplace. For someone just starting out, that's quite a reach.

The reality, however, is that your Etsy shop won't necessarily reach 30+ million potential customers, and you are competing for attention with nearly two million other sellers. Starting a shop on Etsy is simple, but it will only take you so far. Think of it as a great way to test the waters with very little commitment. When you are ready to take your Etsy store from a side gig to a full-time job, you'll want to create your own website. Here's why.

Controlling the Narrative

Branding is an integral part of building a business. As an entrepreneur, you need to figure out how to best tell your brand's story — through both words and visuals. Research shows that 29% of small businesses do not have a website, and 31% "use social media instead." Although social media is important, a website is still the only place you can completely control your brand narrative. While platforms like Instagram and marketplaces like Etsy are powerful tools for increasing your brand's reach, you are always at the mercy of their algorithms and product updates. With a dedicated website, you control every aspect, and are able to establish a direct connection with your customers. Skilled entrepreneur's know this. It's not a coincidence that nearly all top sellers on Etsy have their own websites as well.

Legitimacy & Social Proof

The first thing most people do when they see or hear about something they think they might like to know more about is google it. A brand that doesn't have a website will not only lose out on potential new customers but can also risk not conveying legitimacy. Building a website is so easy these days that there simply is no excuse to not have one.

It may seem suspicious to customers if you don't have a website. The same goes for social media profiles. Your business should be easy to find and engage with on social media. "Social proof" is a very buzzed-about concept that refers to our innate tendency to follow the crowd. It's why the more followers you have, the more likely someone is to follow you, and why influencer endorsements and testimonials are marketing gold. Use social proof to your advantage on your website, by incorporating product reviews, testimonials and press mentions.

The Power of SEO

Building an audience for your brand and getting your products out there is hard work. SEO (Search Engine Optimization) is a powerful tool that if done right can land you at the top of Google's search results for certain terms related to your business. Although Etsy has built-in SEO tools that allows your shop to be found, a dedicated website will extend your reach beyond the Etsy marketplace. Having your own website show up in search results also builds brand awareness and credibility in a more powerful way than an Etsy store.

Extending Your Reach

Creating your own website does not mean that you need to shut down your existing Etsy shop. On the contrary, having multiple sales channels is often a good thing, at least until your business grows to a certain scale. Etsy is an effective way to find new customers and reach a wide audience, so use that to your advantage. Providing potential customers with multiple entry points is always a good idea.

Community & Connection

While it's true that Etsy has a very dedicated following and has been able to build a large community of buyers and sellers, nothing compares to connecting with your customers directly. As an entrepreneur, you are not just managing an Etsy shop, you are running a creative business that happens to use Etsy as a platform to reach customers and sell your goods. Your own website gives you a platform to tell your own stories and build your own community. On Etsy you will always be one of many. Your website will always be entirely about you.

So why don't all small businesses have a website?

Around 25% of business owners say it's because they lack technical knowledge and 22% state it's because they don't have the human and/or financial resources. Those may have been valid excuses in the past. These days, building a website doesn't have to take any longer — or cost much more — than setting up an Etsy store. Your customers are out there, and your job as a small business owner is to ensure that they can find you, wherever they are looking.

WHY WIX AND ETSY ARE GREAT TOGETHER

If you do have your own website, some suggest you close your Etsy shop and give up on Etsy entirely. But given the fact that Etsy brought in over $87 million in the third quarter of 2016 alone, do you really think that's the best advice?

Over 20 million people are active buyer's on Etsy. That's a lot of chances to sell your products. If you're serious about selling online full-time, it should be a part of your business. But only a part.

Instead of closing your Etsy store, why not connect it to a Wix website? This creates a free way to bring traffic to your website.

Wix is a website creation tool for people who don't know how to design websites. You don't need to know a line of code. If the thought of creating a website gives you nightmares, their Artificial Design Intelligence makes it easy. Just answer some simple questions, and in a couple of minutes you have a website.

By combining your Wix website with your Etsy store, you've got a built-in source of organic traffic to your website that won't cost you a dime. Free traffic is hard to come by these days. And when you are building a business on a shoestring, the dimes really add up.

Why Should I Include My Etsy Store On Wix?

If you want a business that will last, you need to build it on your own, not on Etsy. What would happen to your growing brand if Etsy started charging $1000/year to use their platform?

Etsy does an awesome job promoting their brand online, in print and on television. They spend hundreds of thousands of dollars marketing to continually gain new customers. People trust Etsy and love to buy from them. These things may be true about you, but if you have hundreds of thousands of dollars to spend on marketing, you wouldn't need to have an Etsy store.

While Etsy is a great platform that works hard to satisfy both buyers and sellers, it does have limitations.

These limitations make it hard to grow your business. But it is possible to get the best of both worlds. Embedding your Etsy store in your Wix website allows you:

- Easier email list building
- A better customer experience
- The ability to nurture customers who aren't ready to buy
- No links to competing products

1. Easier Email List Building

On Etsy, you only get your customer's email addresses when they make a purchase. This is a great starting point, and you should already be emailing your customers on a regular basis.

But customer emails are only a starting point. This doesn't provide an opportunity to connect with the people who didn't buy on their first visit to your site. With Wix, you can use one of their list-building apps to capture email addresses of your site visitors who aren't yet customers.

2. A Better Customer Experience

Customer service for online businesses starts with a website that makes it easy for customers to find and purchase what they want. Call it user experience, customer service or customer experience. The bottom line is you need to make it as easy as possible for customers to buy from you.

Part of the reason people love to buy from Etsy is they make it super easy for anyone to buy. Search, click, buy. That's it. Why spend countless hours trying to figure out how to do all this yourself when you can just use their process?

If you don't want to deal with setting up shopping carts and integrating them with payment gateways, the Etsy

Store App from Wix takes customers to the Etsy checkout page. Because customers trust Etsy and love to buy from them, your abandonment rates will be lower.

3. The Ability to Nurture Customers Who Aren't Ready to Buy

If you're selling a high-priced item, it may take several visits before they trust you enough to make a purchase. Though there isn't an "official" number from Etsy, sellers figure the average sale price on Etsy at around $20.

If you offer a freebie on your website in exchange for an email address, it will be easier to stay in touch with prospects. This way, you can send them emails that will guide them towards purchasing your product.

4. No Links to Competing Products

When a customer views your item there is a menu that takes them to several products from other Etsy sellers. The Etsy shop inside a Wix website doesn't have these links, so your potential buyer will not have a way to find similar products from a different seller.

CHAPTER 8
MANAGING YOUR ETSY ACCOUNT FROM ANYWHERE WITH WIMAX

When it comes to the digital landscape, nothing has succeeded quite like the world of hawking goods online. And while there are plenty of different auction sites out there, as well as the wild world of Craigslist, there are also other means that are more effective for selling goods at a rate that means making a profit. Nothing has managed to burst out from the scene quite like the craft and vintage site Etsy, where various people from around the world can use wireless internet to sell everything from fantastic Pyrex to graphic t-shirts. And the market has definitely responded, with various trend pieces and other sources spending time talking about the phenomenon that is Etsy.

Anyone who is taking this kind of selling job seriously knows that the best way to rise to the top of legions of web-only stores is staying in constant contact. And for anyone who is willing to invest in WiMax, there's automatically the opportunity to get online and check up on sales and postings from anywhere, not just the spots that happen to have Wi-Fi. After all, part of how it's possible to make money online is staying in contact constantly. And since people who travel and people without reliable Wi-Fi make up a large portion of the Etsy community, the chance to invest in an online service that brings the web anywhere is a chance to make even more of a profit.

The idea of upgrading from typical wireless internet service to something more substantial than cable or DSL is not just a phenomenon that is appealing to those hawking vintage goods online. From start-ups to serious business people, plenty of web users are starting to make the decision to go with a service that goes where they do. And because of this, there is the chance to actually accomplish tasks from anywhere. Organize the shipping of a box while visiting family, or simply take advantage of the fact that updating listings is suddenly possible from anywhere. It's the most responsible way to get things done online, after all, so having a connection that makes it possible is all the more sweeter.

Those who are shopping and who have been sucked into the cult that is Etsy also find that having accessible web from anywhere is a fancy and effective way of keeping up with the other customers who are making bids. After all, it's possible to grab anything from the best Tupperware to a vintage sofa on Etsy, and knowing the preferred shops that stock one's beloved goods is a great way to save money on local flea markets and other sources for vintage goodies. Of course, the chance to upgrade to WiMax means the chance to open a laptop anywhere and check up on chosen shops and other content. Not making the mistake of waiting also means first choice on the best new goods, which is a lot like knowing which day to head to the local thrift store for the latest batch of vintage wares.

ARE YOUR ETSY STORE PRICES TOO LOW?

Do you wonder if your Etsy prices are too low? Pricing is a major element in your Etsy shop's success. Price too high and your customers will just walk away. Price too low and your customers won't take you seriously. What is an Etsy shop-owner to do?

There is a very good chance that your prices are too low. Crafters, particularly women crafters, have a tendency to under-price and under-value their work. Many new Etsy sellers start out by setting their prices just high enough to cover the cost of their "hobby" supplies, so that they can keep doing it. They don't add in profit or a wage for their work in creating the item.

They may also think that if they don't price at rock bottom level, their items won't sell. It is easy to think that if you keep your prices low, you will sell more.

However, this is not the case, at least on Etsy. Etsy is mostly a market of small, handcrafted, specialty goods. (There are also some very large supply sellers on Etsy, but we'll assume that you are not one of those). The shops are closer to boutiques than they are to chain stores.

Boutique items come at a premium, and they should, because they are hand-crafted with individual love and care, and because they are usually one of a kind (called OOAK in the Etsy lingo). A higher price gives an "impression of value"

The rule of thumb for pricing on Etsy: if you want to sell more, raise your prices.

This may seem surprising, but it works.

If your item is good quality, and it is photographed and described well (you can't skip these steps!), then it has value. You are the only one who can communicate its value to the customer, and your price does that. Your price immediately gives the customer an impression of value regarding your item.

Set the price high enough to cover your materials, and an hourly wage for you, and profit.

In addition, remember that it costs 20 cents to list an item, and when it sells, Etsy takes 3% and Paypal takes 1%. Things sold in the $5 range will bring in little money indeed!

When deciding your prices, also look at your competitor shops--the shops that are selling similar items to yours. Find the average of their prices. Start there when thinking about your own, and then go a bit higher.

If you are still uncertain, and afraid to raise all of the

prices in your shop, try coming out with new line that is priced significantly higher than your other items. You may be surprised to see how well it does.

One pricing strategy that can work wonders, and is used by successful sellers, is to feature one very high priced item prominently in your shop. This makes your other items appear less expensive and more accessible, while retaining the overall impression of value in your shop.

Finally, when pricing, remember that even if your Etsy shop is just a place to sell your hobby, it is still a business. Businesses are supposed to make profits Do not be afraid to think about your handmade goods as high quality, one of a kind items that are worth a premium. Of course you cannot forget the importance of gorgeous presentation through magazine-ready photography, and thorough and compelling ad copy in your descriptions. But do all that, and you'll be in a position to make more sales, and more money, from your Etsy shop.

THE NUMBER ONE MISTAKE ETSY SELLERS MAKE AND THREE WAYS TO

FIX IT!

Taking pictures of your items is key, and I believe it's at least as vital as making your crafts in the first place. You've gone to all the trouble to create something which you believe people are going to want to buy -- so you need to put just as much effort into making sure your listing shines! Here are three common mistakes people make and how to fix them:

Blurry Pictures!

The best way to photograph your items is to set your camera on a tripod first. I find yard-sales are perfect for getting cheap tripods. If you're photographing jewelry or smaller items - you can easily pick up a mini-tripod for under $10 online.

If you don't own a tripod, use a couple of hardback books (the dictionary makes a great base for cameras!). The main aim is to keep the camera as steady as possible and if you have a timer on your camera -- try using it to avoid shaky pictures!

Background

There so many people who sell on Etsy, and take quick snapshots of their jewelry/art/accessories draped over carpets, tablecloths and even on lawns! It really doesn't flatter their hard work!

To solve this - get a nice piece of card stock from a craft store -- choose a color which is going to compliment your items (white works well for jewelry) and make sure you have good natural lighting or a couple of lamps focused on your items. Better still, you can make a light box for a couple of dollars, a quick search online will give you plenty of good tutorials. It's amazing the difference a light box can make!

Colors and Sharpness

Finally, make sure you adjust the colors and sharpness of your photographs. If you own Photoshop, then this can be done by running the "sharpen" filter and then adjusting levels and colors. But if you don't own Photoshop and want to do this for free, then a great site to use is picnik where you can upload your pictures and adjust them in a few simple steps to really make them look great.

CHAPTER 9
HOW TO CREATE PASSIVE INCOME WITH ETSY

Assembling the building blocks for your new business earlier rather than later is key. Doing this will make the process of opening your shop easy, quick and stress-free.

1 Choose A Name

While deciding on a name for your Etsy shop, be sure to do a quick search to make sure someone isn't already using the one you are thinking of. Search Etsy, as well as social media to make sure your name is available across all platforms.

While it can be frustrating when the shop name that you have set your heart on is not available, do not let it discourage you. Consider several different shop names options and narrow down the perfect one that no one else has.

2. Do Your Market Research

How to create passive income with Etsy? First, Your Etsy shop does not stay in a vacuum. It is part of a lively marketplace.

So, before you list your items for sale, give some thought to the shops you like best. What are they doing right? What do you think they could do better?

Think about what it is that other shops are doing right, and consider how your shop could do it even better.

How will you stand out and make your own mark in the market?

Also, pay diligence to your opposition and stores selling similar items to your own. You should have a clear idea of what your products will sell for, not just what you feel they are worth.

3 Be A Part Of The Community

Being a 'super citizen' in the Etsy community can take you far.

Engage and participate in the site's forums. Reach out to sellers you admire, and ask for their advice, and offer to promote other shops which you think your customers will appreciate.

Supporting other seller's can help them, and it will also help your own store as well.

Often the audience of your favorite shops will serve as a useful crossover as you build your own. Plus, having support from established sellers will go a long way when you are just getting started.

4 Offer Deals

Offering deals and coupons, especially for your loyal customers will encourage return visits, as well as help build your following!

Often a special sale is just the incentive a customer needs to pull the trigger on an item they have been eyeing.

Furthermore, specials can generate interest during slower sales seasons, and keep customers interested to come back to check on items in your shop.

It's important to keep your shop updated with new products regularly. Keeping your shop fresh with new products lets people know you have a vibrant, active business, and encourages customers to keep coming back to see what's new.

5. Develop An Etsy Business Plan

Take some time to scroll through your competitors' shops while taking note of their products, their price ranges, and anything else that may help you develop a competitive brand.

6 Branding & Design

When your shop has a professional look and feel overall, it builds customer trust and makes an important first impression.

SUCCESSFUL TIPS ON HOW TO MAKE MONEY ON ETSY

If you want to make money on Etsy, the easiest way to do it is to sell your crafts, supplies, or services for custom orders.

Etsy is the go-to marketplace for arts, crafts and everything in between, so it's not surprising that many artists, crafters and other creative people prefer this community over other ecommerce platforms.

Contrary to the most common misconception about Etsy sellers, you don't have to be artsy to make money on Etsy. For one, the company welcomes affiliate marketers (who promote other people's items in exchange for a percentage of the sale).

How to Sell on Etsy with Enough Profit Margin

Like any ecommerce business, the key to success is to sell items on Etsy with enough profit margin (or the difference between the item cost and its selling prices).

If you're planning on opening up a craft store, the cost could mean the wholesale price you got from the factory or any direct supplier. If you're creating your items for sale by hand, then cost means the amount you used in manufacturing the item.

To calculate profit margin, you'd have to subtract cost from the sale price. For example, you made a mermaid tail blanket with materials costing $50. You then decide to sell it for $95. The profit margin is $45.

Your goal as a seller is to increase profit margins high

enough that your Etsy business can be sustained. Here are some tried-and-tested tips to do this:

Always know your gross profit margin. (FYI, gross profit margin is total sales minus cost of items sold). No matter how big or small your business is, identifying this number helps you assess your company's financial health and adjust accordingly if needed.

Be on top of your items' prices. It doesn't matter if you've already decided on pricing for all your items. Sometimes, you have to make the tough call of upping the price for reasons beyond your control, such as increase in materials, change of supplier, and so on.

Bulk vs. Retail pricing is OK. Don't be guilty if you're charging your customers different prices. Enterprises, government agencies, or large companies may be less price-sensitive than individuals who buy retail.

Avoid discounts. Sale and discounted prices are okay occasionally, but if you keep on discounting your items on Etsy, it could quickly damage your profit margins. If you really want to get ahead over your competition, find another non-financial way (such as improving customer service, adding valuable information with each purchase, and so on).

CHAPTER 10
15 REASONS WHY YOUR ETSY SHOP DOESN'T GET MUCH SALES

If you run an Etsy shop there are a lot of things you should think about that have nothing to do with your items. And so there could be a lot of reasons why your shop doesn't have a lot of sales even if your items are really good! We analyzed these reasons and made a list of 15 most important of them.

1. Your titles and tags are not optimized (SEO)

We've put SEO (Search Engine Optimization) on first place in our list for a reason - it is the most important thing for online selling. Without optimized titles and tags your shop's items won't be found by buyers which means no sales.

2. Your photos doesn't show up your products in a best way

Online shopping is all about photos. Of course photos should be clear, not blurry, with good light and details. But it's not just about that. Your photos should not only show up your products as "this is a white shirt with this kind of sign on the front", for example. This is boring and this kind of information you would put in description anyway. Photos, on the other hand, should be more personal, they should call buyers to purchase. Until buyers got a package with their purchase all they have is a picture. And so it should be very attractive picture! If you can get modeled picture it would be great. If you're not sure what would be an attractive picture for your product try to check Etsy search for similar products and see what kind of pictures are on the first few pages.

3. Your products description is not clear

Your product description is very important as well. Even though Etsy states descriptions doesn't have anything to do with their search results, it is still have to be interesting to read, clear and cover all required information about the product. I would recommend to visually divide your description in blocks with paragraphs and use each of them for specific purpose. For example, first will go your description of the product itself, maybe where the inspiration came from, etc. Then you can specify dimensions of the product. In next block you could also mention materials you used, especially if they have some specific properties or might cause allergy. And of course you should also mention care instructions for your product. When you have this scheme for a description try to write all your description in this same way so your customers would know where to look for each detail.

4. You don't have enough items in the shop

If your titles, tags, photos and descriptions are fine but you still have low sales it might be because you don't have a lot of products in your shop. Wide variety of products is good not only so customers would have choice, but it also increases your chances to be found in search and throughout Etsy. The more items you have in the shop the better! A lot of sellers believe that +100 items is the spot where you begin to get regular sales. I would say 100 is first major point, but if you can get to 200 or 300 - it would be even better!

5. You just opened your shop a few months ago

Sometimes it takes awhile to get your first sale. And actually it is so most of the time. Very rarely first sales happens in first week or two. You need to be patient! Remember that it needs time for your items to take their position in search, to spread on Etsy through teams etc. Use that time to improve your descriptions, photos, to create more products. When sales start to grow you might not have time to create new products regularly.

6. You don't have any reviews or you have a bad review rate

If your shop is new the reason you don't get sales might be because you don't have reviews yet. That's a problem and you can't really do anything about it. Buyers just don't feel safe to order from shops without reviews. But someone will trust to order from a shop without reviews at some point, you just need to wait. Then just make sure to point out to your first customers that your shop is new and their reviews are crucial for your business.

Also if your shop rating is bad (you've had a few * or ** stars reviews) this will also affect your sales. One thing that buyers wouldn't trust to buy from you if you have bad reviews. Another thing that Etsy lowers stores with poor rating in search results so less customers visit your shop which result in less sales. If you happen to have bad reviews try very hard to either fix that reviews with customers, or if it's not possible try to get as many reviews as you can on top of that bad reviews so they would "hide" them on your shop page. Of course it will still affect the rating of the shop, but keep in mind that Etsy takes into account only feedbacks left over the past year so at some point it won't matter anyway.

7. You don't promote outside of Etsy

If you don't promote yourself outside Etsy (blog, social pages, local fairs) all your shop visits would be only from Etsy and this is just not enough for a steady sales. You should promote your products everywhere you can online and offline. Regular blog posts and social shares and posts will bring visitors to your shop online. Also always have your business card with you to give it out at fairs and other events. Potential customers who have already seen the product with their eyes are more likely to come back online and buy that product.

8. You don't ship your products internationally

If you don't ship internationally this would also affect your sales number. Just think of all the customers outside your country that can't get your products. To see it in number check your Etsy stats for a wide range of time and switch to "Map" to see all visits from other countries. If you don't ship abroad and your sales are low consider adding international shipping to your shop. It won't cost you much trouble but the number of your potential buyers will grow drastically.

9. Your prices are too high or too low

This might seem ridiculous but both of these statements could be the reason for low sales. Low prices can scare away customers - that's a known fact. If your prices are too low for your category customers might be afraid to buy from you, as your prices just don't seem appropriate for the product. They will expect that there will be something wrong with the item or that you will ship not from your stated shipping address, etc. So if this applies to you try to increase your prices a little and see how this will impact your sales. And usually that helps.

On the other hand too high prices can reduce sales too. It's hard to say when your prices really are too high, it's more like trial and error method. But keep in mind that if you increase and increase your prices comparing to other shops at some point your products might become more of a luxury products. Which means your targeted audience will probably change and you would need to rethink your promotion tactics, your photos, packaging, etc accordingly?

10. You haven't filled up your shop policies

Filled up shop policies are crucial for your shop for a few reasons. Potential customers often check the policies to know what to expect from the seller, how seller handles specific situations (refunds, returns etc.). This is very important to build trust worthy relations between buyer and a seller. Besides, filled up policies is a good safety net for seller as well in case of any trouble with shipping or damaged goods. And another very good point why you should have your policies filled up is because it affects your placement in search results. Moreover, using Etsy's policies template will also slightly improve your search placement.

11. You don't have a wide variety of products in the shop

Having a lot of items in the shop as we said before is good and having a wide variety of products is quite different but also very good for your shop. As a seller you should consider different products (though products in the same niche would be better). This way customers visiting your shop wouldn't get boring with similar or just slightly different products and will visit more pages, therefore you will have a higher chances to get a sale.

12. You don't check your stats regularly

I know a lot of sellers who don't pay attention to their Etsy stats at all and check it occasionally just out of curiosity. But Etsy Stats (and even better Google Analytics) is a very powerful tool. Start the habit of checking the store statistics for at least couple of times a day. This will help you understand where your main audience comes from so you would know what sources you should pay attention to. Also by analyzing your statistics you will see which tags work better for you and which don't work at all, which is very important for SEO. You can also see when specific products start to be popular (seasonal products or gifts for instance) so you can adjust your available quantities and prepare for high season.

13. You don't post cross links in your descriptions

When customers visit your shop from search results, category pages or from Etsy home page they usually get to one product page. You can increase views number for your shop by adding links to your items description that will invite customers to either visit your shop page, or specific section, or even specific item or your shop search result. So with these increased views you will also increase your sale chances. This could be very useful if you sell products in different listings that could be paired and sold together.

14. Your customer service isn't the best

You should always treat your customers nicely. The power of mouth is huge and if you are not polite or not really trying to satisfy your customers that might have a bad impact on your sales. This also can result in bad reviews which will worsen situation too. Just remember that good customer service always pays back!

15. You don't prepare your products in advance

As they say, a spoon is dear when lunchtime is near. You should always keep in mind that customers often buy products for specific occasions way in advance. So basically you need to prepare your Christmas products starting summer and your Valentine products starting autumn. That's normal and if you sell on Etsy for awhile already you might have noticed that some Christmas themed products start to appear as soon as in July. It might help to create a calendar for most popular occasions and mark dates when you should start working on them and dates when you should start listing them on Etsy.

Of course it is also necessary to take into account the quality of the goods, speed of work, if your products are widely present on market, products demand, etc. But these are 15 major reasons why you might not have a lot of sales on Etsy... yet. Check all of them, work on some points if they apply and soon you should have steady sales.

CHAPTER 11
3 REASONS SELLING DIGITAL DOWNLOADS ON ETSY LIMITS YOUR GROWTH

1. Minimal Branding Options

The upside of the simplicity of the Etsy platform is the ease in getting started. Because all stores look essentially the same, you can focus on your product descriptions and images, making it totally possible to start a new store in a matter of minutes.

Make Your Store Stand Out

While this simplicity is helpful when first taking the step of building the store, it can quickly become a downside as you begin selling digital downloads on Etsy. It is incredibly difficult to make your store stand out in a marketplace of identical storefronts.

Etsy will advertise similar products on your page, making it dangerously easy for interested customers to click away and lose your store in the shuffle.

When selling digital downloads on Etsy, you want potential customers to focus on your product, not be distracted by items from other sellers.

When creating your own site, you have significantly more control over your click funnel. Building a beautiful, eye-catching storefront is easier than ever before, so with only a little more time, you can put together a professional-grade store that establishes a degree of trust with potential customers.

Keep in mind that selling digital downloads on Etsy (or anywhere) generally depends to some degree on the personality behind the product.

2. Limited Marketing Opportunities

One more time with feeling: repeat business accounts for 40% of sales. Retaining customers is vital to surviving in the digital marketplace, but it is significantly more difficult on larger, more anonymous eCommerce hubs.

Brand Recognition

Think of it this way: do you remember the name of the

store where you last bought a product from Amazon? Have you asked a friend where they bought an accessory and gotten the response: "from Etsy"?

To be successful online you need referrals and customer engagement, and for that to happen, you need a memorable, easily accessible site, ideally with a unique URL.

Targeted Marketing and Discounts

Features like list-building, abandoned cart emails, and customer info retention let you keep an eye on both individual and broader shopping habits and reach out to your customer base in a more specific, targeted way- i.e. offering discounts for repeat shoppers.

Etsy is not built or integrated with platforms for this kind of tracking and engagement.

Customer Contact Information

Through targeted messaging, you can create customers who not only come back for more, but end up promoting your store to their friends (cool, huh?). This is possibly the biggest drawback to selling digital downloads on Etsy and truly limits your growth potential.

Search Engine Optimization

Additionally, SEO is huge for bringing your store to new eyes- another Etsy no-go. When you create your own online store with Selz, you can add multiple pages and a blog to the site free of charge.

This means you can create content and pages that lead brand new users to your site through SEO and targeted advertising. Without this strategic inbound opportunity, you are essentially banking on how Etsy chooses to show your listings and how users are searching for products.

Multichannel Selling

In a nutshell, a store focused around digital downloads needs a combination of word-of-mouth, good marketing, and solid internal mechanisms to thrive. Control over your brand, messaging and customer engagement is what leads businesses to thrive.

Etsy makes the process of getting started simple, but from there you're pretty much a small fish in a big, distracting pond.

3. High Fees and Subtle Added Costs

On the surface, Etsy seems very affordable- and starting out it is. Because there is no monthly fee for use, and just a small charge to list new projects, getting going on Etsy is incredibly cheap.

Over time, though, Etsy's fees can add up and take out significant chunks of your revenue.

Etsy takes 5% of the sale price for every item you sell, plus checkout fees (another 3%), meaning that 8% of every sale goes directly to Etsy.

Again, early on, when you are only selling a few items a month, this isn't a huge cost. The more inventory you move, however, the more this ends up costing. For example, if you sell an eBook of recipes for $20, $1.60 of each sale will go to initial costs. Sell twenty copies in a month and you're already up to $32.

But, there's more. The 5% transaction fee now also applies to the cost of shipping, which can put a significant dent into your overhead, especially if you're shipping larger items.

PROS AND CONS OF USING ETSY

Etsy is a marketplace started in New York, whose primary focus was and is on handmade items. Many do not realize that Etsy allows its users to sell handmade items, vintage items and supplies for crafting.

The idea of Etsy is to provide viable alternatives to shop locally and sustainably. Buying handmade over mass-produced items is another achievement that Etsy has brought to the marketplace. Vintage items must be at least twenty years old. Commercially produced items will generally only be tolerated if they are in the supply category, for use in making your handmade or craft items.

Pros of Etsy

Perhaps the number one pro of this marketplace is that it has been an outlet for crafters and artists to debut their wares to the world. This has paved the way for many people to work at home or develop a home based business.

The second pro would be that it can provide exposure for your handcrafted item. Many sellers are featured in a series by Etsy which are called "Quit Your Day Job" which proves that they have turned a small time craft into a business. Some artists have been picked up by local galleries or had their items debuted in museums. Others have had their items offered in boutiques. Some seller's reported they were selling more online than in their brick and mortar shops, and closed their real stores to have the luxury of working from home with low overhead costs.

The third pro, would be that it's cheap to use allowing for the start up of a small business to be painless on the budget. Etsy's fees are in comparison, lower than most online storefronts. Currently and since inception, you obtain a store for free. A listing with five photos has since inception costs twenty cents for four months. Selling fees are inexpensive also, and Etsy has remained on top of the marketplace since inception. Recently they have implemented their own checkout system, so that sellers can avoid using PayPal.

Fourth would be ease of use. It is a very uncomplicated system where the screens for listings prompt you though each step.

Fifth would be finding local items. Selling locally to those who want to shop local is very easy and can connect you with local buyers.

Last, but most importantly would be the Etsy community. Many refer to Etsy as "Pleasantville." Their rules of Etiquette make it a "nice" place to be part of. Like minded sellers can network with others in online forums, obtaining support from the Etsy staff as well as peers. Many sellers report they have made friends with local crafters in their neighborhoods or worldwide connections that they would have otherwise forfeited.

Cons of Etsy

The cons of using Etsy are more prevalent now than in the past. Due to all the pros, so many sellers have opened up shop on Etsy meaning the marketplace is flooded with items.

Sellers report that it's hard to make their items stand out. A new jewelry seller may be going up against almost four million handmade jewelry listings at any time. Vintage sellers may find that their shop consisting of fifty to one hundred items is just a small spurt in the millions of Vintage items that may be listed on Etsy at any time.

Others may open up a shop on Etsy for "fun" and not

for business, clearly not realizing the work that goes into running an online store. Selling on Etsy is hard work and should be treated as such.

CHAPTER 12
ORDERING INVITATIONS ON ETSY - ENSURING A POSITIVE OUTCOME FOR A HIGH QUALITY END PRODUCT

Please keep in mind that Etsy is just a marketplace/platform where a shopper can find things from thousands of shops worldwide. This means that you are not actually ordering invitations from Etsy, but rather from an Etsy shop/vendor.

Etsy got it's reputation for a great place to order invitations due to its established original invitation shops. Those shops opened between 2005 and 2009. The invitation designers from those shops took great pride in the work they provided their customers and still do. However, starting around 2010 hundreds of "new "invitation shops began to open on a daily basis. In an effort to gain customers and compete against the established reputable shops, many began to sell invitation designs at an extremely low price. "Cheap" invitation shops have taken over the Etsy search landscape. While established and reputable designers charge on average between $15 and $25 for an exclusive personalized invitation design, these "cheap" invitation shops are selling invitation designs in the range of $5 to $10 each.

When you factor in a graphic designer's time, Etsy seller fees, PayPal fees, and listing and relisting fees, a shop selling a design for $5 to $10 is not making a profit - not even a minimal one. Most do experience high order volume and live off the "cash flow" due to the large order volume but the gross receipts and expenses subtracted do not equal a profit. There is no genuine interest other than to rack up enormous quantities of sales and live off the cash flow.

Unfortunately, many customers want something at a very low price but the ages old saying still remains true - you usually get what you pay for. If a vendor is selling a design for $10 or less be sure to look at the tips listed further below. A red flag is a newer inexperienced shop desperate for sales willing to "give away" their designs and work by selling at an unbelievably low price.

Concerns over some of these types of shops:

Lack of graphic design experience

Many of these shop vendors have NO graphic design experience

Inappropriate design software

Some are using unprofessional software - such as web-based applications or even Microsoft Publisher (these will never create a high quality graphic design product

Do not include bleed margins

Many do NOT have any idea about working with "bleed margins". If your invitation design file does NOT include a professional bleed margin, you will be in for a big disappointment when you print the invitations - there is an unavoidable automatic thin crop which takes place at print time? If the file does not have the bleed margin, critical parts of the design and/or words/text may be cropped off at print time.

Low resolution print files

Blurry/Pixelated/Fuzzy Invitations. Because of inexperience of just lack of graphic design training, you may receive a file in low resolution which may look great on your computer screen or smart phone (all computer images are low resolution so they load fast) - but will NOT print out crisp and clear and may not even print at the correct size.

TIPS FOR AVOIDING DISAPPOINTMENTS

If a vendor is selling a design for $10 or less be sure to look at the following factors shown below before placing an order.

1 - Look at the Date the Shop Opened

How long has the shop been in business on Etsy? (Verify the years)

2 - Look at the Number of Sales They Have Had and notice if they have been active in the last year (the more sales they have had over the course of multiple years - chances are you are in good hands)

3 - Look at the Shop Reviews

While every vendor is entitled to have some negative reviews just because of the fact that not every customer can be pleased, look at the overall average number of Stars

Anything 4 to 5 Stars - Probability is that you will be in good hands. Anything below 4 Stars - Keep shopping - you will be better off in the long run.

The BEST picture of a shop owner's reputation is created by looking at all 3 factors Combined. The Shop Owners who have been Multiple Years on Etsy - especially over 5 years PLUS significant number of Sales PLUS a Great Feedback Average - You should feel comfortable doing business with them.

WHAT IS ETSY'S SELLER PROTECTION POLICY?

Etsy Seller Protection offers assistance to eligible sellers in the event of a dispute with a buyer.

To qualify for Seller Protection, you must comply with our Seller Protection Policy and remain in good standing with Etsy. Good standing means that you:

- sell qualifying items
- ship orders on time

- respond to Conversations in a timely manner

Seller Protection and Etsy's case system

Etsy's case system is a platform for buyers and sellers to work together to resolve concerns about orders. If you and a buyer are unable to settle the issue on your own, the buyer can ask an Etsy specialist to step in and mediate the case.

The specialist overseeing the case will determine if the order and your shop qualify for Seller Protection. It's important that you respond to Etsy's requests for information in the case log within the time frame given by Etsy to prevent action from being taken on your account.

After the specialist has reviewed the dispute, they will either provide you with specific directions to resolve the dispute, or may issue a refund for the order if you have not complied with Etsy's policies.

The Seller Protection Policy doesn't guarantee a resolution in your favor, and it doesn't indicate that Etsy's Service Level Standards (our expectations for customer service) were met. Sellers who don't comply with Etsy's policies are subject to review, which can result in suspension of account privileges and/or termination.

CHAPTER 13
HOW TO SELL ON ETSY WHOLESALE

Despite increasing competition, with trends pointing toward authenticity, local and unique—Etsy might just be the brand that wins hearts and wallets." However, the standard Etsy platform is really only right for specific handmade goods, and it lacks access to bigger retail platforms looking to buy at scale; these buyers are on Etsy Wholesale, however. So for many sellers, Etsy Wholesale is a better choice.

While your website is the home of your online store and brand, Etsy Wholesale is a great place to validate products and see what sells, scale and reach new customers and audiences.

Eligibility for Etsy Wholesale

To be accepted as a seller on Etsy Wholesale, you must meet several requirements. First, you must offer wholesale pricing, defined as 50% or less of the suggested retail value, which itself must match the current retail prices on your website.

There is a 3.5% transaction fee on all purchase orders you will need to agree to. The fee structure is different for large retail partners like Whole Foods or Macy's, with a fee of 10%.

Second, Etsy will review your record for customer service. They do this by looking over your Etsy reviews and compliance with their policies; if you don't have an Etsy shop, they can judge your website and other online indicators of customer service. Finally, Etsy will assess your "overall professionalism." For Etsy Wholesale, this means having strong, consistent branding and an appealing aesthetic throughout your online store, and a good assortment of products.

There is a 3.5% transaction fee on all purchase orders you will need to agree to. The fee structure is different for large retail partners like Whole Foods or Macy's, with a fee of 10%.

Second, Etsy will review your record for customer

service. They do this by looking over your Etsy reviews and compliance with their policies; if you don't have an Etsy shop, they can judge your website and other online indicators of customer service. Finally, Etsy will assess your "overall professionalism." For Etsy Wholesale, this means having strong, consistent branding and an appealing aesthetic throughout your online store, and a good assortment of products.

Apply for Your Etsy Wholesale Account

In your application, you will need to give Etsy details about your business, your contact information, number of employees, clarify which category or categories you'll be selling in, provide production details for your goods and agree to the wholesale pricing policy.

Onboarding Process

Once Etsy approves you, it's time for the onboarding process. Go to Shop Manager And select Add channels on the left at the bottom. Click on Continue Wholesale setup. To get your wholesale shop rolling, you need to pay a one time $100 fee, confirm your credit card on file, add at least one wholesale listing, and fill out your profile and policies. Since there are lots of pieces in the onboarding puzzle, we'll take them one step at a time.

Set Up Your Linesheet

You need to list at least one thing on your wholesale linesheet to get your Etsy Wholesale store moving, but the linesheet can stay hidden until you want to publish it. You can add existing Etsy listings from a standard store, or you can create new wholesale listings by clicking on Add a listing.

It's free to list wholesale items, and you can deactivate or delete unwanted listings after publishing. For maximum impact, try showing the item photographed as if it was in a retail display.

Remember, all items on your linesheet must reflect an Etsy Wholesale rate—at least 50% off your retail prices on every other platform, including your website.

Set Up Your Policies

You can set up your policies once you've listed at least one item. Set all of your policies before you create your profile.

First, choose payment methods. This is easy, because Etsy Wholesale only accepts Etsy Payments. This means buyers can only use credit cards right there on the Etsy Wholesale site. You can accept other payment methods such as PayPal, credit cards through Square or even checks off the platform and then mark your PO paid. (You cannot, however, meet a buyer on Etsy and then bypass the platform and sell the buyers the items through your website to avoid the fee.)

Set your payment policies including tax terms, payment deadlines, and your cancellation policy. If you decide to offer net terms (the option for buyers to pay you the balance within 30 days, for example), put those terms here. If you ship before you get paid, Etsy will not reimburse you should your buyer fail to pay.

The default understanding on Etsy Wholesale is that there are no maximum quantities a buyer can purchase, so if you have limited quantities of an item for sale, mention this in your listing. On the other hand, you can and should set either a minimum order requirement (MOR) or minimum order quantities (MOQ), the minimum a retail buyer must purchase to get your wholesale price. Buyers can't split the MOQ between items; for example, if your MOQ on a listed pair of slippers was 10, a buyer would have to buy 10 in each size. Etsy Wholesale encourages a MOR of $200 to $300; if you're using a MOQ instead, they recommend setting the MOQ so it's in the same range.

Include your shipping method here, including costs, delivery speeds and carriers. Let buyer's know the variables, such as weight or distance, that might affect shipping cost. Also include information about production time and time before shipping.

Include any other details here that have to do with shipping and fulfillment. For example, while you can consign with buyers on Etsy Wholesale, the platform is not optimized for this practice, so you're basically on your own.

Set Up Your Profile

Your Wholesale profile is similar to an "About" section on the main Etsy website, so look at your favorite sellers there for inspiration. Tell your brand story and the origin of the store. Use striking photography and well-designed graphics; this is the place to capture new buyers with professional, beautiful images. You can use five business images, in .gif, .jpg, or .png format, each at least 812 pixels wide, 428 pixels in height. You can also use video.

Provide details about the business so your buyer's feel like insiders. Show them what makes your brand unique. This is the virtual "meet and greet" for your brand and store. And of course, provide your contact information. The public can't see your address — just the city. Include links to your website, social media pages and blog.

Publish and Integrate with your Website

Once you've set everything up, publish your linesheet. It's accessible to all approved Etsy Wholesale buyers. Now, promote your Etsy Wholesale store on your existing blog, social platforms and website.

Add calls to action and links directing buyer's to your Etsy store right on your Weebly website so everyone can see your products on the new platform. If you use Google Analytics, make sure your CTAs are on your top-performing pages. You should also integrate in ways that feel natural; a link to your Etsy Wholesale store "feels right" on your main store page, or on a blog post about holiday shopping, for example. You can even make your positive feedback do double duty by linking reviews of your products on social, on your website, and elsewhere online to your Etsy Wholesale site, and vice versa.

HOW TO BLOCK A BUYER

Since e-commerce is all about sales, products and customers, all online sellers tend to search for new ways to reach a bigger audience. Less often they think about how to diminish the number of their customers. Usually, they do not think about negative sales experience or unpleasant buyers. However, there are situations when sellers have no other choice than to block a buyer.

How to block a buyer on Etsy?

Basically, it is a system that consists of a few basic steps that will result in you blocking any kind of Etsy user. In other words, it does not matter if they are sellers or buyers. Basically, you can even block those who are following you. After doing this, they will be unable to see your actions in their feed.

If you want to block someone on Etsy, you have to go to their profile page. Then, all you need to do is click on the "Block" link, which is at the bottom left. The important thing is that they won't be notified about your action.

How to unblock someone on Etsy?

Do not worry if you accidentally block someone on Etsy, because you can unblock them whenever you want. Also, they won't be notified about any of these changes.

When you decide to unblock someone on Etsy, in order to do that you have to visit their profile. Toward the bottom left you will see the "Unblock" button. Once you click it, that Etsy account will be unblocked. There are no restrictions for blocking or unblocking a certain account.

CHAPTER 14
THE DO'S AND DON'TS OF SELLING SUCCESSFULLY ON ETSY

So here is by no means a comprehensive list but a good start...

DO Answer 'convos' politely and promptly, I think it is great to add a bit of humour be yourself even if it is the tenth person that week asking if you would like to giveaway a cushion on their blog. You can say "No thank you" nicely. This includes being polite even when people ask you questions you have answered numerous times in your policies, listings and shop intro. For example, "can I get the cushion without the insert?" I probably get asked this at least once a week despite it saying on every listing that they come without the insert.

DO Always have your shop looking tip top! You never know when you will be featured in an Etsy finds email or on the front page or maybe even on a popular blog. So if people are coming for the first time it may be the difference of them giving you a heart and returning later or not.

DO Always have high res images ready (if you load pictures onto flickr that will help as you can download any sizes) for magazine editors or bloggers who may be interested in featuring you.

DO Follow Etsy's rules.

DO price accordingly. Include Etsy fees, Paypal fees, packaging and stationary, plus the time it takes to list the item, take photos etc, package it all up, take it to the post office plus the actual making of the item, material costs, time taken to get these materials, time taken to actually make it… what are you prepared to work for?

DO think about how to market your product. What makes it unique? Why would someone buy it? When people buy from you what are they buying? For example when someone buys a cushion from me they are buying a souvenir. They are buying the memory of a lovely holiday, the place they went on their honeymoon, the town they grew up in, the place they met their partner. They are buying something eco friendly.

DO look at your product critically. Is it original? Do people get excited when they see it? Is it unique? Can you get it anywhere else? Does it appeal to a wide range of people? I am lucky that my products appeal to women and men and people also buy them for kids too – know who you are selling too and market accordingly.

DO have postage listed to lots of different places, and make sure it is accurate. Do not make money out of postage, put your prices up if you need to. There is nothing worse than receiving something that cost you $10 in postage to have it say $2.20 on the envelope. Take the items to the post office and get them weighed.

Do have all your shop policies filled out. How long will you reserve items for? What about returns? What about if an item doesn't show up? What are the postage times?

DO check your convos regularly. I have heard people say "I have a life I don't want to be chained to the computer all day." You don't have to be, but you do have to check your emails at least 2 times a day I think. You have to allow for time differences.

DO take a really good look at your shop. Look at it from a customers perspective. Does it look neat and tidy with all the sections filled out and all the photos looking nice? Really, does it? Is it full of lots of items so you show up in searches a lot. Are you items in sections so people can easily find what they want? Have you used every tag for every item?

DO BRAND EVERYTHING: when someone buys a cushion this is what they get:

There will be no confusion as it to where it came from, so people can tell their friends about you too. Put your logo on shop name on everything!

DO have your shop announcement filled out: it doesn't have to be a huge amount of writing just a little bit about the products, same with your profile, just a little bio about yourself, why you started making what you make, what materials you use.

DO have lots of detail in your listings and your item title. Who would this be a good present for? On what occasion would you buy it for someone? How can it be used? How is it packaged – say if you are selling artwork people want to know it is going to arrive safely. How big is it? Put the size in cms and inches. It drives me mental how many people put a coin next to the item to show size? How would i know how big a coin from another country is? Are all the tags filled out – every single one?

Now, for the flipside…

DON'T Spam your customers… don't send them loads for convos/emails one to say you received the order and have posted it is suffice.

DON'T Feel like you need to have a facebook, twitter, blog, and instagram account before you can sell anything. All of these things can be very useful but they do take a bit of time to get the hang of and can be done as you go along.

DON'T Put a bad photo on Etsy, you may be tempted to quickly list something but it may be the difference between a heart and a future sale or nothing. Are you photos looking tip top – with the help of some free photo editing like snapseed? Just changing the colour contrast and brightness will make a huge difference you want your pictures to really pop off the page. For example having the cushions on a chair etc but others swear by this so you will have to decide what works best for you.

DON'T Leave bad feedback without discussing it with the shop owner first. Be reasonable, this is someone's business. If someone does leave you bad feedback you can use the Etsy kiss and make up feature.

DON'T COPY!! I see people blatantly copying the work of sellers who do really well – orginal is best. Always. And people will know you have copied and think that is not very good.

DON'T obsess about the number of sales. Yes there are shops that have sold 10 000 items +++ but why worry about them? You cannot compare your shop with other shops that sell different products to yours, so don't.

WHY MOST PEOPLE FAIL AT SELLING ON ETSY

Selling on Etsy is not easy. It is not simple, and it is not a get rich quick scheme. It is a selling platform which can be used by those with enough drive to jump in and try.

They don't have an etsy shop plan

This doesn't have to be fancy. Mainly it just needs to include your customer avatar, that is the person you intend to sell to. Who is your audience, what does your ideal customer look like?

It would help if you also mapped out your time – how long it takes you to make one of your items, how much you will sell it for.

How much time do you have to spend working on your shop and also making your items? Clarifying how much or how little money you will make. It's worth doing from the outset. Otherwise, you could end up working for 4p an hour.

Your marketing plan – how will you promote your

shop. If you are only planning to use the Etsy search SEO, which is excellent in the beginning. How will you maximise each listing to get the most out of search?

They don't have a business plan

As above a business plan is your overall plan for your business. Similar to that above but goes outside your Etsy shop. What tools will you use, how much will services cost, postage, packaging? Will you use outside platforms to promote your shop, what will this look like?

Listing one item and hoping for success

Yes, there are exceptions. I'm sure there are shops out there with 13 items listed and make a full time living.

However, this is not the norm. I'd suggest at least 50 items before you start to see any traffic, 100+ ideally.

100 items is a good number for giving you extra insights into what is selling, what is seasonal, and what can be extracted and made into a new listing.

You might also get ideas on what to list next and what to try out. All beneficial if you want to make a full time living on Etsy.

They think they have something unique

You've just listed your beautiful item on Etsy and are happy with the photos, the SEO and the overall appeal. Then you have a quick search for your keywords and find that not only has your item already been 'done' it's like a plague of them, but it's also all been done before.

Don't despair. This is perfectly normal and part of the process of selling on Etsy.

What will make you unique is taking your idea and making it better, slightly different, more upmarket, better photography, larger, an extension of a best seller.

This process is especially true in categories like planners, or printables. However, if you are selling earrings made from paper and milk, you won't need this angle.

They forget to invest

Basically, at the end of the month, you pay yourself a percentage, and everything else goes back onto the business either in training or investment.

If you are making things to sell in your shop or designing items you've already invested in a sewing machine, or pens or even a computer.

All an investment in your shop. What you need to do is invest in only those things which will make more money. So you might spend on a course to help you market your shop.

You may invest in a badge machine, so you don't have to make them by hand, allowing you to speed up and sell for more profit.

They don't work hard enough

Not all shops have to work hard in order to make sales on Etsy, there are a few shops which despite appearances don't really 'do much'. Ever stalked the stats on your sweet competition.

CHAPTER 15
HOW TO SELL PHOTOS ON ETSY

Selling photos on Etsy is a great way to promote your work in a new marketplace and earn money at the same time. Many photographers use this as a way to earn extra money. Others treat it as a full-time job.

Physical Prints

People love hanging art on their walls or buying small prints of stunning landscapes. Prints are also great gifts for friend's and family. Best of all, they're always in demand, regardless of time or season.

Selling physical prints comes with a lot of logistical and design-related challenges. Before you can sell prints in this form, you need to make sure the shipping fees aren't overwhelming.

You can limit the countries you sell prints to. This will also limit the number of buyers you have.

You also need to make sure that the printing/framing company (or printer) you use is trustworthy and will create photos in the best quality possible.

If you want to take this even further, make sure you have a lot of packaging options available. If you go the extra mile for your clients, you'll impress them. And inspire them to visit your store more often.

If you juggle these tasks wisely, you'll be able to draw in a lot of clients without breaking the bank.

Digital Prints

If you don't want to worry about logistics, you can sell digital versions of your photos. Users will get a download link to your photo as soon as they purchase it.

This is perhaps the easiest and fastest way to make money on Etsy. If your photos are striking and are accompanied by the right keywords, your business will inevitably attract a lot of buyers.

Copyright rules are very important when it comes to digital files. Make sure you have a note in your description stating what users can and can't do with your photos.

In general, photographers allow printing and prohibit commercial use. You can let users know that you're okay with commercial use as long as they credit your work or pay you an extra fee. It's completely up to you.

Photography Resources and Textures

Some photographers sell photos of different textures. Users can turn these into prints or use them in design or photography projects.

Resources are very popular. Like Lightroom presets, they can enhance a simple image. If you take sharp and appealing photos of textures, you should give this option a shot.

You can also sell presets or actions to help photographers further enhance their images.

Photo Books

This is a fantastic option to showcase your work in one book. Again, you can sell this in the type of ebooks or real physical duplicates.

In the event that you don't want to create a simple photograph book, you can write a guide accompanied by your photos. You can also create a book filled with in the background photos or inventive stories.

Photograph books may not sell as fast as normal photo prints. Be that as it may, they're an incredible way to show off your creativity and teach photographers something new.

DO ETSY SELLERS NEED A BUSINESS LICENSE?

Whether or not you need a business license to sell on Etsy depends primarily on whether you're treating your Etsy store as a legitimate business or just a hobby. To help you decide whether you need a business license, ask yourself the following questions. If you answer "yes" to any of the questions below, you'll likely need a business license in order to operate legally.

Cheat sheet: Do you need a business license to sell on Etsy?

Are you making a profit on Etsy? If you're buying and selling on Etsy without making a profit, you probably don't need a business license. However, as soon as you start making profits, you're required to report your profits to the IRS. Many sellers ignore this rule and don't file income on their profits. If caught, these sellers could face fines or be required to pay back taxes.

Are you operating your Etsy store as a business or a hobby? While the IRS gives vague guidelines on how to judge whether your store is a hobby or for-profit, here's the summarized version: If you're doing it for profit, it's a business, not a hobby. Businesses will be required to get the appropriate business licenses in order to operate legally.

Is your company a partnership or LLC? If you've formed your Etsy store as a partnership or LLC, you'll be required to get an EIN for your business, as well as the requisite busines licenses.

What business licenses do I need to sell on Etsy?

If you are operating your Etsy store as a business and turning a profit, you'll be required to play by the same rules as any other online seller. Just because you're selling on Etsy instead of your own website does not exempt you from getting the appropriate licenses.

The 3 most commonly-needed business licenses for Etsy sellers:

A basic business operation license. This is a permit that allows you to operate your business within the local government's geographical jurisdiction. The license requirements for operating a business vary by state and by city, so your best bet is to contact your local Small Business Administration office to ask what permits are required in your city. For ecommerce merchants, the licensing requirements are usually minimal, and the application costs are usually between $50 and $100 (although this varies by city and state).

An Employer Identification Number (EIN). An Employer Identification Number is how you'll report taxes to the IRS. If you've registered your business as a sole proprietorship, which is very common for Etsy sellers, you aren't required to get an EIN since you'll report taxes on your personal tax returns. If you've formed a partnership or LLC, you'll need an EIN.

Home Occupation Permits. If you're operating your business out of your home, you may be required to get a Home Occupation Permit. For most online merchants, this isn't much of an issue, but if you're making your products out of your home (as many Etsy merchants do), you might need this permit

Is it safe to sell on Etsy without a business license?

Only if you're running it as a hobby, not a business. While many large sellers continue to sell on Etsy without the appropriate business or tax licenses, they're risking being caught by the IRS, and they may be susceptible to local or state fines as well. Our advice is to make sure you have the appropriate licenses if you're serious about building your Etsy store into a real business - mostly because we don't know of many people that have tangled with the IRS and come out on top.

As long as you're not operating your Etsy store as a legitimate business and aren't making profits, you don't have to worry about getting a business license. In other words, hobbyists, crafters, and other casual Etsy users (which comprise most of their sellers) don't need a business license. If you're attempting to run your Etsy store as a legitimate, profitable business, you will need to report your income and get business licenses. If you're just starting your business and aren't sure if it's profitable yet, you can use the five-year exemption to postpone having to decide.

Pro Tip: The Five-Year Exemption

Even in case you're working your Etsy business for profit, you can choose to have the 'revenue driven assumption' made after 5 years of business operations rather than right away. What this means is that you can operate your business for the initial 5 years without the IRS deciding whether your business is for-profit or not by documenting structure 5213 with the IRS. On the off chance that your business is profitable 3 out of those 5 years, your business will be ruled for-benefit and you'll be required to make good on back regulatory expenses on your income for that period. You can submit structure 5213 inside 3 years of your first year of working the store. This will give you a fairly huge testing period for your online business - if you aren't ready to turn a benefit, your business won't be considered (or taxed as) a for-benefit business. Not exclusively will this allow you to operate without documenting business charges, however, you can also deduct a lot of your independent venture expenditures, so you'll typically set aside cash.

5 THINGS EVERY ETSY SELLER NEEDS TO KNOW ABOUT SALES TAX

Compared with Amazon or eBay, Etsy maintains a small-time, homegrown feel, thanks to its emphasis on unique handmade goods.

The platform and its sellers are doing big-time business, though. In 2017, gross sales on Etsy exceeded $3 billion. In fact, Etsy is large enough that it has started to automatically collect and remit sales taxes in some states that have marketplace facilitator laws — just like Amazon and eBay.

If you sell outside of those states, however, collecting sales tax might be your responsibility — whether you're doing big business on the site or just starting out. Below are five things you should know about sales tax on Etsy.

It's on you to figure out if you have to charge sales tax in a particular state. It all boils down to whether you have nexus, or a substantial connection to a state. That used to mean having a physical presence, such as an office or employees. Today, however, many states now have economic nexus laws as well, which require businesses to collect and remit sales tax if they exceed a certain threshold for revenue or transactions in that state. To learn more, see our post on how out-of-state sales can impact your business.

Before you start collecting sales tax, you must have a sales tax permit. It's illegal to collect sales tax without a permit — so if you have nexus in a state, you'll have to follow the steps to apply. The process can be different depending on the state, and sometimes a fee is required.

Etsy will add sales tax to your listings — but you have to tell it to do so. The platform has a sales tax tool that allows sellers to specify a tax rate by state, individual ZIP code or a range of ZIP codes. However, you need to find the applicable rates and set them up in your account. New listings will have that tax rate applied automatically; for listings created before you set up the tax, you'll want to check to make sure the items are marked as taxable and that the rate is applied. Remember, sales tax rates do not always adhere to ZIP codes.

You might need to add tax to shipping or gift-wrapping services. Some states require businesses to include shipping and/or gift wrapping in the taxable amount. If you don't know the rules and regulations of the states where you have nexus, you might not be collecting enough tax — a situation that can lead to an unpleasant (and perhaps expensive) surprise. So do your research. Once you know whether to apply tax on shipping or gift wrapping, Etsy makes it easy to set this up on your listings.

You still need to file your own returns. Etsy will break down your transactions for you and tell you how much sales tax your business has collected, but in most states, it's your responsibility to remit and file returns. (In marketplace facilitator states, you only need to file returns, since Etsy automatically remits the taxes on your behalf.)

Etsy's small-batch sellers

According to a 2013 Etsy report, selling is a full time calling for only 18 percent of the site's makers and crafters. Thirty-seven percent sell on Etsy in addition to holding down a full-or part-time work.

The normal Etsy seller takes in somewhat under $1,500 per year (based on Etsy's first quarter 2015 financials announcing $531 million in revenue made by 1.4 million dynamic venders).

In the event that you are one of Etsy's many small-scale sellers, you may discover it challenging to do everything your business requires on top of working in other roles that help butter your bread. Building your Etsy business requires buying supplies and making your products, keeping your Etsy listings crisp, and shipping out requests to clients. Over all that, you still need to discover the time to record the same quarterly sales tax returns.

Small is beautiful when it comes to nexus

It used to be that being a small seller kept your nexus worries at bay. You have sales tax nexus in any state where you have a physical presence. For most of the crafters who sell on Etsy, the only point of nexus will be the location of their home or studio.

What is "nexus" and should Etsy seller's care?

Your quest toward fully understanding sales taxes on Etsy begins with identifying where you have nexus.

Also called "sufficient physical presence," nexus is a legal term that refers to the connection that a seller has with a particular location. If a seller has nexus in a state, they have to follow sales tax regulations in that state.

For most Etsy sellers, identifying where they have nexus is as simple: If you live and do business there, you have nexus there. This is enough for most Etsy sellers to know, since the site is filled with home-based artists and craftspeople.

However, there are cases where a seller develops nexus in a location other than their home state. Here are some questions to ask yourself to determine whether you have nexus in a different state.

- Have employees or "helpers" from another state?
- Store inventory in another state?
- Ship from another state?
- Sell goods regularly in another state?

HOW TO SELL PRINT-ON-DEMAND PRODUCTS ON ETSY

But if you've always thought Etsy is just an online

store for crafters and vintage sellers it's time to revisit those preconceptions. It is in fact relatively simple to set up and sell your designs as print on demand products on Etsy!

Etsy connects artists with customers around the world, the focus of the platform is selling unique products that aren't available in big-name retail stores.

Amongst the handmade gifts and vintage items, there's plenty of room for print-on-demand products. Here's why:

-
- People are shopping for unique designs- check!
- Quick and easy shipping- check!
- A good range of products- check!

Why Etsy?

In 2013, they expanded their definition of 'handmade' and started allowing sellers to offer products made by outside manufacturers, with a few of T&C's of course:

The outside manufacturer must meet Etsy's standards.

- Sellers must create the designs for their products.

- Sellers need to prove their involvement in the creative process.

- Sellers must be transparent about their products and how they're made.

These T&C's shouldn't stop any legit print on demand merchants, because any proof Etsy needs on the authenticity of your designs- you should already have! (And let's face it, it's in your best interests!)

Etsy makes positive steps to ensure all the products sold on their platform are authentic, so nothing is copied or mass produced. Providing proof of your involvement in your designs just helps to combat anyone else being able to take them.

CHAPTER 16
INTERNATIONAL SELLING ON ETSY

In recent years Etsy has become the standard selling platform for creatives, and is used by artists, jewellery makers and clothing designers (to name but a few) to successfully market their products to a huge market.

If you're a regular seller on Etsy, have you considered widening your net and shipping internationally? It's a straightforward process, and you could be reaching millions of potential customers in no time at all. The numbers speak for themselves:

-
- Etsy operates in 83 countries
- There were 33 million active buyers on Etsy in 2017
- 70% of Etsy sales are made in the US

Top international markets for sellers

When you sell using Etsy you don't need to limit yourself to the domestic market. Shipping companies will deliver your product (almost) anywhere in the world and tracking services will allow both you and the buyer to follow the shipment all the way.

The main markets you should be considering if you are selling out of the UK are Europe, North America and the Asia Pacific region. While the US is the most mature market with the most buyers, Europe and the Asia Pacific region are seeing strong growth in Etsy sales too, so to overlook them would mean missing out on potential sales.

How to change your profile to international settings

If you're currently restricted to selling in your home market, being able to sell overseas will mean updating your profile settings to become an international seller. This is very easy to do, just follow these simple steps:

- When making a new listing go to Shop Manager and click "Listings" and then "Add a Listing"

- Locate the shipping section and enter your

rates (or let Etsy calculate them automatically)

- Fill out details including places you're willing to ship to, expected delivery times, product dimensions, and domestic and international fees

Select "Save as Shipping Profile" so you won't have to repeat the process with other listings

To ensure your potential buyers can understand what you're selling, you'll need to make sure any text related to your products is translated. This couldn't be easier and there are two ways to do it. To select which languages you'd like your items and shop information translated into take one of the following approaches. Firstly, if you have the translated text, you can manually translate your listings by going to Shop Manager > Settings > Language and Translations. When you've added one you'll be able to enter text in that language.

However, you don't even need to manually translate as Etsy has an automatic translation tool, meaning international browsers of your shop will see a machine-translated version of the text. It's probably not 100% accurate, but on Etsy it's usually the images that sell the products.

Maximise your international sales

So, you've managed to get your first international buyer. Congratulations! What next? There are some areas you'll need to get right to ensure everything goes smoothly and you end up with satisfied customers and a healthy profit.

To avoid extra charges or even returns, make sure you've measured and weighed your package correctly and have paid the right tariff for sending it. One top tip here is to invest in a set of scales that will allow you to accurately weigh your products (and don't forget to include the weight of any packing materials too).

Customs/tax pitfalls to avoid

If you're sending goods to another country make sure you fill out any customs declarations forms in the right way. You generally don't have as much control sending a package internationally as you would domestically, so the key to success here is to minimise the risks. You can do this by using a reputable firm that offers tracking, such as FedEx or DHL, and filling out any associated paperwork correctly.

Never mark your item as a 'gift' as this can cause problems if it is held up by customs, and is actually illegal if the item has been sold.

Generally speaking, if you're sending packages to the US, items with declared value of under $200 will require no additional paperwork, but anything with a higher declared value may be inspected and a duty or tax imposed on it. Buyers will usually be responsible for any extra charges, but it's good practice to make sure they know this in advance and make your shipping conditions clear on the Shop Policies page.

HOW TO SELL ART ON ETSY

Put resources into your photos. Photos on any online store do much more than just showcase your item – they speak to how truly you take your business and the overall quality of your products. Invest in a good camera, learn basic photography methods and take plenty of photos for your shop. Of course, not everyone is a persuading picture taker. Only half of the Mousesnaps team knows her path around a digital camera. In the event that you can't seem to take good photos, enlist the help of a companion who's more skilled or has a superior camera. A lot of amateur picture takers will be willing to take photographs on the off chance that you offer them a photo credit on your site.

Stage your postings. When you post a new thing on Etsy, it's listed at the top of the relating area for a short period of time. This gives you and your store increased visibility. Each time Mousesnaps has had a major sale or inquiry, it's been immediately after another posting. On the off chance that you have a few items to transfer, it makes sense to space your postings over a period of days to boost your exposure.

Take advantage of classifications and tags. Etsy's suggested labels are there for an explanation – they're common things people look for on the site. Use Etsy's suggested language instead of your own. For example, if you're selling a set of kitchen towels, be sure to use the "towel" tag. Don't skip that tag and instead create your own "kitchen towel" tag – you will miss anyone who comes to the site and just searches for through the towel tag. In the event that you have available labels left for your posting after, you've selected any appropriate ones Etsy has listed, feel free to make your claim.

Leverage your personal systems. Cross-promote your Etsy posts on your Facebook page, your blog, or Twitter (Editor's note: I'd likewise include Flickr. People go looking for images and see your stuff). Etsy even has a toolbar highlight that lets you share your new listings on Facebook if you're signed into both sites. However, keep at the top of the priority list that no one likes to be marketed to all the time – so make certain to keep it entertaining for those in your systems. Don't only tweet when you're posting a new thing. What's more, don't update your blog once every week when you're adding something new to your store. Keep people involved in your business by posting anecdotes about your creation process, giving an inside look at something as its being completed or just keep people up to date on your related endeavors. It's considerably more fascinating that way.

Selling Art on Etsy Isn't That Hard

Do the math. Calculate the cost of your materials, your time and Etsy fees to price your products appropriately.

Don't just pick a round number because it sounds good. Also – be honest with yourself about how much you're charging. A good way to test the quality of your product against your price is by going to a flea market or craft fair and setting up a booth. People will be brutally honest if they think your product is overpriced. And similarly, if your product is flying off the table, you know you can raise your price.

Check out the competition. Routinely patrol Etsy for sellers who are making your product or something similar. Are they cheaper? Does their product look better? Adjust your listings so that you're competitively priced. If you think you have a superior product, explain the difference in your product descriptions. Remember what we said about the photos – appearance is everything! Make sure your store has an awesome shop name, too.

Love what you do. It sounds so corny, but you have to like what you're doing to be successful. It's a real shocker that the two of us love mousetraps so much – but it's true! We've had huge orders come in and had to drop plans and paint all day and night to get them out. It was strangely fun for us, so we know we're on the right track.

CHAPTER 17
RUNNING AN ETSY STORE IN COLLEGE

Finding an employer willing to extend this type of flexibility can be challenging; luckily, the internet opens up all kinds of possibilities for entrepreneurs of all ages and all career stages. If you have the ability to produce your own handmade products, launching and running an Etsy store could be an ideal way for you to help fund your college education and start your career in ecommerce at the same time.

Running an Etsy store during college can be done on a low budget, from startup to operations and marketing. Many colleges provide the internet and Wi-Fi service needed to run an online store. Fellow students may even be interested in helping you with marketing, production and order fulfillment so you can grow your store and earn even more toward your schooling.

As your online store takes off, you can take advantage

of working capital loans if you find you need to rent space, buy inventory or scale production in advance of the holidays and other busy selling seasons. In addition, the experience you gain in owning your own business, managing people and what you learn about ecommerce could be the start of a promising career as an entrepreneur.

Add more channels

Put your store into the shopper's path, instead of waiting for shoppers to (somehow) discover your Etsy store. When you manage stores on multiple platforms, instead of just one, you'll reach more shoppers. Some of the other platforms where you can run online stores alongside your Etsy store include:

Bonanza – Whose tagline is "everything but the ordinary." This platform was voted the best place to sell online by more than 12,000 sellers.

Zibbet – Home of more than 52,000 independent creatives which promises unique, one-of-a-kind products that will amaze and inspire.

Handmade at Amazon – Where handcrafted, one-of-a-kind products can be found for sale right alongside millions of other products on the world's biggest ecommerce platform (you can also earn revenues as an Amazon Associate in the form of commissions on sales driven through your online links).

Ormalize your schedule

If you were working for a local employer you might have flexibility, but you'd still be required to show up on time, stay for a shift and complete assigned responsibilities. You need to adopt the same mindset while running your Etsy store while in college.

Set hour's for work time – both the time needed to run your Etsy store and to produce the products that will be sold on it. Write down a list of responsibilities and tasks that you'll complete each day, week or month, and hold yourself accountable to fulfill it. Remember that your store's success hinges on your willingness to put in the time needed to promote and run your online store.

Master Seo

Consumers are savvy and many are tired of the same-old, same-old. Whether they found a mass-produced item online that inspired a search for handmade alternatives or saw something they wanted at a craft show, boutique gift shop or a neighbor's home, they know they can turn to online search to find items similar to the ones they want. The better you optimize your product and store pages for online search, the more buyers will find your stores instead of similar competitors.

Build your contact list

When buyers who are interested but not quite ready to buy find your Etsy store, your ability to capture their email address or earn their follow on social media could be the single most important thing you can do to contribute to future sales. Contests, giveaways, easy-to-follow links and pain-free registration processes can all help you grow your contact list more quickly.

Prioritize publishing

It will take time to manage and run your Etsy store from an operations standpoint, but you can't stop there. Establish a formal publishing schedule for social media and email marketing to increase brand awareness and create opportunities for future sales to both returning and first-time customers.

Plan to scale

Every business plan should include contingencies for what to do when sales slow or when sales begin to exceed production capabilities. Your college may even have startup incubator programs or be willing to let you use a vacant classroom, dorm or other space to house production capabilities on an on-going basis, or temporarily during busy seasons.

Running an Etsy store could be your ticket to paying for schooling and achieving financial independence before you've even earned your degree. Use these ideas to launch your own store or find like-minded students who want to partner with you as internet entrepreneurs.

5 REASONS TO KEEP YOUR DAY JOB WHILE STARTING YOUR ETSY SHOP

But there are pretty awesome benefits to keeping your day job until you can stay on your own two feet that cannot be overlooked, despite our excitement and wanting to dedicate 100% of our time to our new Etsy shop.

1. You get a consistent salary with benefits.

Being self-employed is hard, and it's financially risky. There's taxes and accountants and bills to be paid, and unless your shop has been making a consistent income there's never any guarantee that you'll be able to pay them next month.

Even if you do get a consistent income, there's always weaker months or standstill months and the bills just keep adding up.

Top it off with the fact that you have to pay your own medical insurance, nobody covers your sick days or off days, etc. And you'll find yourself in a financial struggle if anything happened to you while you're still in the process of building your business.

2. No Stress! (well, mostly no stress)

Did you know that chronic stress is linked to 6 of the leading causes of death?

Gee, that's a bit morbid.

But really, stress is a silent killer and nothing is more stressful than running your own shop, especially in the beginning (aside from having a kid. Or twelve.) Your 9-5 usually has a time limit. You finish, you go home, you're free.

Your shop however is like those zombies in Legend, it never tires of bugging you, never lets you rest peacefully and eats away at most of what you own.

3. Build your empire at your own pace.

No pressure, just build it one day at a time. With stress removed and no financial disasters looming over your head, you're pretty much free to grow it in your own pace rather than running a rat race where sleep deprivation is taking over every good cell in your brain. You can go as fast or as slow as you like, work when you feel like it.

4. Your coworkers (I know, I know)

I know most coworkers aren't your best friends.

But even if they are just a kind face that greets you in the morning, that's more you're going to get as an entrepreneur.

Especially since we're dealing with online customers, this would be our only interaction with anyone that doesn't live with us.

Of course, you don't have to be a part of the statistic and you very well can go to the coffee shop to work, but with long, unconventional working hours you're bound to get lonely at some point (unless you're home with the kids like).

So while I bet you never thought to stay at your work for your coworkers, enjoy it as long as you have the option to - you'll miss company culture one day.

5. You get to look sane for another couple months

To conclude, yes, there's many benefits to quitting your job, but there's also downsides to it and keeping your job might be the logical thing to do (even if the passion is burning in your heart).

And I know that it might not be easy to hear, but I want to tell you what everybody else doesn't. Sometimes it's okay to put the dream on low burner while you take care of your finances, your home, your life and just build your dream as you go.

How to talk about your etsy shop on linkedin

So, you're working on revamping your LinkedIn and have no idea if it's appropriate to talk about the Etsy shop that you've put your blood, sweat, and tears into. I mean, who wants to hear about the sixty different soy candles you've crafted?

WHY SHOULD I PUT MY ETSY SHOP IN MY LINKEDIN PROFILE?

Speaking about your Etsy shop is on LinkedIn can be a huge differentiator because it showcases a combination of your entrepreneurial spirit with an individual passion of yours (well, let's trust that you're energetic about whatever you sell on Etsy). It gives something for people to identify with you by demonstrating a piece more about your character than what's just on your continue.

So, how can you show off your Etsy shop in a way that impresses recruiters or whoever else is popping by your profile to stalk your career 'cred?

Except if you're running your Etsy shop as a full-time job (and if you are, props to you—that's amazing!), it might be a tad needless excess to make a whole experience section for your shop. In this case, the Projects section is going to be your friend! You can add a new project to your profile.

Here are some ideas for what to include:

A connection to your shop (doh!)

How long you've been running your shop for you?

The type of item you sell. Don't worry in case you're a doctor and you sell little dog toys—it shows you have interests outside of just work! This also gives individual a easy way to start a genuine conversation with you.

Stats that you're glad of (for example of sales in x amount of time, of unique visits, transformation rate)

Any methods that you've learned and used that you feel proud of (cough hack mastering Etsy's own breed of SEO).

Don't forget!

Beyond just adding a project for your Etsy shop, don't forget to add the skills you've learned along the way to your skills section. This could include things like Search

Engine Optimization, Keyword Research, Customer Service, Analytics, and much more!

You can (and should!) also include a link to your Etsy shop in the links section at the top of your profile. Who knows, your next big order or dream client could find you through LinkedIn, so it's best to show it off in as many places as you can (within reason).

All in all, it's likely that selling on Etsy has given you a ton of attractive skills and experience that should certainly be shared. Taking time to outline and describe what you've achieved on Etsy will not just give you a little certainty boost and kick in the butt to expand your store even more, however in case you're on the job chase, it'll make your profile shine some extra and plan you to talk about this key highlights in possible future meetings.

www.ingramcontent.com/pod-product-compliance
Lightning Source LLC
Chambersburg PA
CBHW060834220526
45466CB00003B/1099